D0207140

THE BEES OF RAINBOW FALLS

Finding Faith, Imagination, and Delight

in Your Neighbourhood

Preston Pouteaux

Urban Loft Publishers | Skyforest, CA

The Bees of Rainbow Falls
Finding Faith, Imagination, and Delight in Your Neighbourhood

Senior Editors: Stephen Burris & Kendi Howells Douglas
Copy Editors: Marla Black & Frank Stirk
Graphics: Amber McKinley
Cover Design: Roberta Landreth

ISBN-13: 978-0-692-87309-0

Made in the U.S.

Praise for

The Bees of Rainbow Falls

This is a charming book, and unique. Taking his interest in beekeeping as both an illustration and a metaphor, Preston Pouteaux calls us to embrace the long, slow, beautiful work of cultivating neighborhood. *The Bees of Rainbow Falls* calls forth attentiveness, presence, kindness, and courage, the very qualities required to re-posture ourselves towards others and change how we see the places where we live.

> -Michael Frost, author, *Incarnate* and *Surprise the World!*

What do beekeeping and learning to love your neighbours have in common? "Everything!" according to this delightful and engaging book by my friend and colleague, Dr. Pouteaux. Through personal stories and reflections, fascinating historical accounts and challenging texts and images, Preston encourages and urges us all to re-imagine where we live as the place where God is at work and where we are invited to join Him. Read it and read it again, share it with others and most of all, live it!

> -Karen Wilk, author, *Don't Invite Them To Church*

This book is a lot like Preston - it is gentle and interesting and engaging. His writing is both profound and humble, and nudges the reader to engage and be curious, without ever feeling coercive or forced. It is unusual to find modern writers who ask questions and write with the simple elegance and unpretentiousness that Preston does. He has the power to make his reader feel cared for and significant - actually loved. This is exactly the sort of empowering and encouraging teaching that the world desperately needs from today's church. I hope it will be the first book of many.

> -Lyndon Penner, author and popular gardening radio columnist

Preston Pouteaux is curating a fresh conversation in Canada by stepping into the neighbourhood with a beekeeper's attention to the small and the beautiful. He embodies a love for his city and is a compelling example of how the Church today may truly live as those who love God and our neighbour.

-Alan Hirsch, writer and leader in the global missional movement. alanhirsch.org

There are many who write well and get around to some of what they write about, but Preston lives this out well and has finally gotten around to writing about it so that many who will never be able to see it, can imagine it through this wonderful book. There are very few that I know who come even close to seeking "Shalom" in and for neighbourhoods as Preston does. This kind of life is needed in neighbourhoods across our land.

-Cam Roxburgh, Executive Director of Forge Canada

What an enchanting read! *The Bees of Rainbow Falls* reminds us that community outreach is far more than a matter of programs, strategies, and mechanistic solutions. Rather, it is a magical adventure of joining God where he is already at work in natural, everyday ways. This is a delightful invitation to experience the true beauty of being on mission with God.

-Rev. Michelle Sanchez, Executive Minister of Make and Deepen Disciples, Evangelical Covenant Church

You, like me, will be captivated with the fluidity and revelation in Preston's book. However, more so with your newfound passion and understanding for the person in your own Rainbow Falls.

-Eric Samuel Timm, Orator, Author, Artist, Visionary

This book is dedicated to Peter Beermann,
my kind and patient beekeeping mentor,
and to Lake Ridge Community Church,
our beautiful band of neighbourhood-loving Jesus-followers.
You are beloved.

Table of Contents

Foreword

Most people travel through their lives blind to the beauty and possibility all around them. Like the ancient story of Jacob's ladder, they require special interventions before they awaken to the sacredness of a particular place and exclaim, "Surely God is in this place and I was not aware of it." But, what if you could strike the match? What if you could turn up the receptivity channels? What if even your most ordinary moments became the windows to meaning and goodness?

The delightful book you are holding is a light switch. Yes, the writing ignites creativity. Yes, the storytelling curiously draws you in. Trust me, you will buzzing about bees before the end. But there is something else! Subtle adjustments are made on your focal lens chapter by chapter. They sneak up on you. By the end you will see differently. Creation, neighbourhood, YOUR LIFE - none of these will be the same.

It is not so much that the reading makes your everyday moments extraordinary (although some may take on this quality). It's more like drinking a glass of water when you've been in the desert for days. The "ordinary stuff" comes alive with the goodness and value it is meant to hold. The bicycles, the barbecues, the barbershop, and of course the bees. Every dimension of your parish will take on an enlivening power.

I love exploring neighbourhoods where the Good News is becoming visible in a tangible way. You know, places where the wall of division between people of difference is coming down. Places where peace, beauty, love, and grace are emerging through the struggle. I'm talking about communities where people are awake to what God is up to in their place and they seek to join in. These are parishes where friends live out their faith together in visible and compelling ways - where loving God, and loving neighbour are as central to life as they were to scripture.

My work with the Parish Collective has taken me into over a thousand such neighbourhoods, walking the streets, entering shops, and sharing meals in homes. There is an awakening happening, on-the-ground in real places. People are opening up to a whole new way to be human, and it is making a difference in concrete and grounded ways. Preston's book helps unravel the mystery of this awakening. It helps you understand what is at play in this growing parish movement.

What is the secret to such a book? What gives Preston Pouteaux the keys to unlocking such hidden reserves of abundant life and relational goodness?

I've known Preston for many years and I have watched the kind and generative ways that his life has fostered beauty, healing, and friendship both in his neighbourhood and in the world at large. Visiting the Pouteaux Botanical Garden and Apiary (also known as his yard), walking Rainbow Falls (his neighbourhood), visiting gatherings at Lake Ridge Community Church (the church he serves), or learning from his wide-ranging newspaper articles, books, and workshops - I have begun to learn the source of his joyful imagination.

What is the secret? I say it is this: Preston writes as a man whose imagination has been set free from the illusion of independence.

This is important to say, not just because of how rare it is to meet someone who is not trapped by this illusion, but because it gives good reason as to why this book is such an unusual guide. Most books on the subject of faith and neighbourhood address various ways of living and engaging that will work well for changing other people. You know - how to reach them, how to help them, how to get them into your church - sort of books.

This book is a surprise. The focus is the other way around. It centers on how God used the neighbourhood (all the relationships, including the bees) to transform Preston's life. The wonder of it all is the way Preston's most personal revelations seem to be the most potent source of help for me, the reader. As the great spiritual writer Henri Nouwen once said, "Anyone trying to live a spiritual life will soon discover that the most personal is the most universal, the most hidden is the most public, and the most solitary is the most communal."[1]

Contrary to popular sentiment, this awareness of our humanity - our need for God, for one another, and for the created world - is not a hindrance to possibility thinking. On the contrary, the exploration and acknowledgement of one's need is precisely what is capable of opening up our vision and setting us free. Preston has learned this lesson, and in deeply embodied and communal ways. This is why he sees differently. It has awakened him to possibilities and practices that fill life with beauty and possibility.

Nobody likes to feel vulnerable. In fact, much of Western society has been built in such a way that we never have to face our need for others, and our connection to the rest of creation. We have taken elaborate efforts to create a world where we can feel like a god. Our food and clothing do not come from the land and animals, they seem to come from a package in the store. We have no need to collaborate with neighbours because our livelihood doesn't come from growing good relationships of giving and receiving; it seems to come from making good money. We have built an entire infrastructure that fosters the illusion of independence.

The great living philosopher Alasdair MacIntyre wrote with astonishment about this distancing from our dependence. "These two sets of related facts, those concerning our vulnerabilities and afflictions and those concerning the extent of our dependence upon particular others are so evidently of singular importance that it might seem that no account of the human condition whose authors hoped to achieve credibility could avoid giving them a central place. Yet the history of Western moral philosophy suggests otherwise."[2] Very little has been written about something so central to humanity.

But Preston's curiosity got the best of him. He stumbled on the secret to recovering a convivial imagination - an imagination that fosters healing connections and a joyful life. Two things happened. Two things that you and I would do well to remember exploring this book:

First, Preston got caught up in the mystery of creation. He became entranced by green gardens and buzzing bees. This was the secret door to the recovery of many truths that had been lost, many life-giving practices that had been forgotten.

Once that first door opened, it triggered the second door. Preston saw his neighbours, really saw them. Not only did he see them, he started seeing the connections between them, both the ones that needed to be celebrated, and the ones that had been disconnected and needed recovery.

Preston began to grow a vision for the ecology of relationships in the everyday life of the parish. Just as he had a role to play in the health and life of bees in the backyard, so also he had a role to play in the healing and flourishing of Rainbow Falls. Once those two doors opened, a whole new way of being developed for Preston. I think the same can happen to you.

This book is your guide to getting those doors cracked open. Get a group together to read and experiment with the practices. Share stories of your experiences and talk about what comes up. Take a posture of prayerfulness as you read and practice together. Trace the pathways back to loving God and loving neighbour. Like Preston Pouteaux, may your life take on new horizons of meaning as you recover the path to becoming a "Keystone" person (don't worry, you'll find out what this means as you read).

Paul Sparks
Co-Author of the award-winning book *The New Parish*
Co-Founding Director of the Parish Collective

Introduction

The grass in our yard was a carpet of glory. As a young boy there was nothing better than playing in its lushness on long July evenings. It smelled like heaven and felt even better. Our backyard was a grassy paradise framed by mom's vegetable garden and strawberry bushes water-fed from dad's own special five-gallon-pail-irrigation-system. "It waters from the bottom so that the roots are forced to grow deep," he'd say. Grass was really my father's specialty. He grew up on a farm in southern Saskatchewan and eventually became a 'professional agrologist' which for me really meant that he knew exactly what a lawn needed to grow. The right combination of fertilizer and care would do the trick. Years later when I bought my first home, he printed off his one-page guide for growing the best lawn and I stapled it to the wall of my garage just above my own lawn mower. As a boy I remember that he would mow the lawn in a precise pattern and my sister and I would run along behind the lawnmower, laughing and staining our bare feet green. I was eight years old when the movie, 'Honey I Shrunk the Kids' came out. It fed my imagination with a whole new perspective for the world around me, for my backyard, and all that lived and moved in the small corners of my mother's garden and my father's lawn. I would lie on the grass, face down, and imagine the world that must be living just beyond my view. I went from being a boy running on the grass to some minuscule adventurer exploring down in the turf below my feet.

My imagination was where I first worked out who I was, what I believed, and how I would respond to the world. Who would have thought that rolling in the grass with my sister would set the foundations for caring for my family, or that burying my face in the lawn would be the catalyst for nudging my little mind towards big ideas about faith and delight, hope and adventure?

Beautiful, life-giving, and heartbreaking experiences shape our imaginations. What takes root in our minds shapes what we see. Our imaginations become almost entirely formed by what we believe about ourselves and others; our lives soon become fully ordered around these realities. What we feed our imagination fills our arteries with adrenaline and hopeful delight, or leaves us lethargic and afraid. Some pursuits are so self-absorbing that many narrow their imagination down to a pinhole of loneliness. Pain and sorrow can be so overwhelming that we find damaging ways to avoid them. We become numb to them. We hide, forget, lock up, and go it alone. The good news is that these places of despair are not the end of the story. What we believe about the world may lead us to push others away, but an epiphany of the imagination may lead us down a new path to see and embrace others with newfound love and joy.

Several years ago I experienced a backyard epiphany that came from a very unexpected place. During a challenging time in my own life, and through a series of unlikely events, I found myself staring into the home of 20,000 bees. Before me was a small world of buzzing insects, working together, creating life for themselves, and pollinating flowers and trees for kilometres around. In one instant I felt as though I was looking at a microcosm of something much more profound than I could yet understand. This brief first encounter became a pivotal moment of imagination-shaping, one that would lead me into the neighbourhood to see others with a newfound sense of purpose.

Looking back and seeing where my love for bees and my neighbours has brought me, I believe that God was taking me on a journey. The God of love, this Gentle Father, intentionally showed me something very important. God knew that I needed to see God's world in a fresh way. Where I once learned life-lessons as a boy peering deep into my father's thick lawn, I was now a man being introduced to a whole world that existed right before my eyes. God wanted me to delight in what He took great joy in creating.

God called me out into the garden. His garden.

The story of humanity begins with a garden, with a gardening God. It's odd to think of God in this way, a dirt-under-the-nails botanist, tending to seedlings, perennials, and bramble patches. Right at the start of the Bible we get a picture of God strolling through the Garden of Eden. He was probably doing what gardeners have done for millennia, pointing out the new growth, breathing in the subtle floral aromas, and admiring the work of his hands. It's no surprise that God invited Adam and Eve to come alongside and garden with him - to plant and tend and delight in flourishing life. Famously, that story did not go well. Adam and Eve were eager to go their own way. Their journey marks the long languishing path that humanity has taken. Relational brokenness is the hallmark of this post-garden world. God's invitation back into the garden is an invitation back into relationship and a return to life.

One of Jesus's most dramatic teachings is that we are to love the Lord our God and love our neighbours as ourselves (Mark 12:31). These are dramatic because Jesus actually calls these the most important commandments. They rise above all else. Here Jesus puts God and neighbours side by side, inviting us to love them both. Loving God seems obviously central to the life of faith, but neighbours? How do they factor in? In my reality, neighbours were incidental to my life, a happy byproduct of living in a neighbourhood. Yet here was Jesus teaching that true life was wedged squarely between love of God and love of neighbour. Out of these two, everything else would sprout and grow. God's domain of grace, hope, redemption, and life exists in this place where our love of God and love of neighbour converge. It was the place where Jesus was inviting me, but first he had to turn my imagination to see the world as he saw it. He needed to reorient my imagination.

When God brought me out into the garden apiary, he was doing what love has always done - God was opening the window of my imagination to catch the fresh cool wind of the world that God was creating before me. God was showing me more than bees and flowers, he was leading me into a place and to a people. God was leading me into the garden of my neighbourhood.

My own neighbourhood is a suburban development called *Rainbow Falls* in Chestermere, Alberta. When we were about to move into our neighbourhood my imagination was full of green trees and laughing children. In my enthusiasm I had built up a picture of new beginnings set against the green and rich backdrop of a thriving new community. But what I saw when I stood on the front step quickly replaced my dreams. Instead of a world framed by shrubs and the smell of freshly cut lawns, my home was set among piles of gravel, covered in blowing dust. Mental images of kids on tricycles and happy families walking their dogs were replaced by loud construction equipment. This was not what I expected; it was ugly.

But this gardening God who set the world in motion saw something that day that I did not. Where my imagination led me to despair, God knew differently. We were placed in this story-less, history-less, under-construction-dust-covered development with an imagination for something more. We were being called to live in a place and be the people who spot goodness, foster life, and tend to beauty. I could not have known that a shy wave to a neighbour was the beginning of a friendship, or that a tray of small perennials, several stick-thin trees, and a small beehive were about to become the start of a new story and a new imagination that would extend to my whole neighbourhood and city. This gravel-dust suburb, *Rainbow Falls*, was a garden waiting to flourish.

The Bees of Rainbow Falls: Finding Faith, Imagination, and Delight in Your Neighbourhood is an invitation to reorient our imaginations towards our neighbours and our neighbourhoods. It is a resource intended to reposture ourselves towards others by renewing how we see the places where we live. Or to put it a better way, this book is intended to help make visible the invisible around us, and help us respond to what emerges. Many of my own imagination-shaping experiences and epiphanies happened face down in my dad's grass or elbow-deep into a beehive. I hope that the stories and insights you find here will inspire you to step into places that set you up for discovery and to see the world around you with new eyes.

This book is in two parts. Part one explores the connections between honey bees and my journey into the neighbourhood. It reflects on how bees have shaped my own imagination and offers insight into how honey bees have been formative in helping other people for thousands of years to see their own neighbourhoods anew. Part two offers six key themes that have emerged in my journey into the neighbourhood. *Beauty* explores how we are being awoken to the world around us. *Awe* reignites our awareness of the sublime. *Security* challenges our sense of safety. *Boring* is an embrace of those small tedious moments of life. *Taste of Place* is about how your neighbourhood is unique in all the world. Finally, *Curates* teaches us the value of caring for what we see. Throughout part two of this book, I've included practices that help 'make visible the invisible,' shaping the way you see your life and neighbourhood with new lenses. They may be thought experiments, interesting postures, hands-on activities, or resources. Loving our neighbours, like beekeeping, is always a moving, living, and complexly beautiful dance of love and discovery. I hope that *The Bees of Rainbow Falls* will serve as a set of waypoints for your journey into your own neighbourhood, finding inspiration to foster new life borne out of new perspectives and a fresh imagination.

I write honestly from my own perspective, one of faith in God's shaping work in my life, as a gardener and beekeeper, and postured towards my neighbourhood. I am a pastor and write with my faith community, *Lake Ridge Community Church,* and my own neighbourhood in mind. I love Chestermere and those who are working for the betterment of our growing city. My allies in this work, and conversation partners in this dialogue, come from varied backgrounds, but we share this deep and abiding sense that we are called to love our neighbours and 'garden' together, trowel to trowel, to create beauty and goodness right where we are. I deeply value their diverse perspectives and I am so grateful for their encouragement to share my own.

This book is a gesture and a nod towards the future of Christian Spirituality, a hopeful re-engagement with God in the neighbourhood. *The Bees of Rainbow Falls* is a reminder that our Faith only thrives when it is snuggly rooted between "loving God" and "loving our neighbour." As the Church finds new footing in the places where we live, orienting our lives towards the story that Jesus is unfolding all around us, I believe we will not only be more faithful, but we will find a richer life of faith.

Part One:

A Honey'd Neighbourhood

Slowly, slowly

"Probably the most dangerous thing is impatience."
-A letter from Eugene Peterson

When I saw the inside of a beehive for the first time, it took my breath away. Thousands upon thousands of working honey bees a mere two feet from me, I froze for a moment. It's a natural instinct. I hope you get to experience it. But for me, in that instance, I was wide-eyed. Without missing a beat, as smooth as butter, my beekeeping mentor was calmly prying the sticky wooden boxes apart to look deeper into the hive. Peter wasn't fazed, he kept working gently and carefully. Peter Beermann is a retired beekeeper who grew up in Central Europe and today spends his winters hand-building beehive boxes. Not only were the bees his, so too was their home. He made it. He knew every smooth turn of the woodenware and his fingers found the edge of a frame. He pulled the wax comb up, covered in hundreds of bees. "Move slowly, or the bees will teach you that you must move slowly," I remember him saying. It was like Yoda teaching his young apprentice. The fact that I knew precisely nothing about the bees didn't seem to matter much to him when we first began. Watching him work with the bees was the first step in helping me move past my own fears - to take a deep breath and trust the completely foreign world sweetly buzzing before me.

Years later, Peter's words ring in my ears every time I open my own beehives.

"Slowly…slowly."

I had just finished my doctoral studies when Peter first took me out to see the bees. My brain felt full after feeding it 10 years of book-work. I needed something else. I needed to experience something that brought all that I had learned about pastoral theology into a new kind of focus. God knew that I needed to breathe, and so God did something that I now see as perfectly fitting the loving character of the Father. He took me to the place where God must take many of his children; he took me to the garden. He showed me the flowers, the roses, David's phlox, and honey berries. He reintroduced me to soil and sunshine and to the rhythm of the seasons and the patience of growth. And there among all the thriving undergrowth, among the flowering apple trees, was precisely the thing that I needed to see: my Father showed me the bees.

God was, of course, showing me more than bees. I was being brought alongside God to see the world through God's eyes. The Maker of heaven and earth was showing a young apprentice, wide-eyed with fear, the beautiful world before us. The Father knew every turn, every flaw, every sound and smell of the world He made, and I felt as though God was taking me into it anew. Away from the books about the faith, God was taking me into the sensual garden all around me, a hands-on crash course of the best kind. To the flowers and the bees, but also, as I would soon discover, to the garden of neighbours, community, and church: to people.

After several seasons of attending to my bees, I discovered somewhere along the way that bees no longer made me nervous. I don't freeze anymore when I open up the hive. Today I'm inspired. Honey bees, thousands of them, live in my backyard and travel all across my neighbourhood of Rainbow Falls. They make things beautiful. They pollinate plants, which create healthy gardens, which make hundreds of other plants and insects and critters happy. Even my neighbour once came bounding over. "Never had an apple tree produce so many apples, ever!" Today when I sit on the bench beside my bees, surrounded by Nanking Cherry bushes and our wall of Scarlet Runner Beans, I see the beauty of these little insects. But more than the bees themselves, I've come to see anew God's work in my neighbourhood.

On the first day that Peter showed me the inside of the beehive, all I saw was a mass of frightening bees. I had no clue what bees meant. But Peter did. Where fear and lack of experience blinded me to what was buzzing about at our finger tips, Peter saw a whole world of life and hope.

It seems to me that Jesus saw so much more when he walked along the shore of the Sea of Galilee. He saw the big picture when he called his disciples from the rocky water's edge. "Follow me." But the disciples were afraid. What about their parents? Their fishing business? The wine at the wedding? The centurion's daughter? The raging sea? The pagans? The Pharisees? As Jesus first showed the disciples his Father's world, you could almost hear the disciples catching their breath, frozen with fear. You can taste their apprehension at nearly every turn. Yet Jesus knew differently. He had experienced the Father's world since the very beginning. He knew of the brokenness, of the sin, of the raging sea, and of the worries. Jesus also knew of the slow, patient, trusting, eternal, present, small, and wonderfully all-encompassing scope of God's domain. He was there from the start. Having shaped the foundations of the world with his Father the Gardener, Jesus was tender in just the right way with his followers. He moved slowly, gently. Jesus knew the smooth wooden edge of Peter's boat, and his fingers found the familiar grip of Peter's hand when he was first helped aboard. In time Jesus's stories and actions all pointed to a world that he wanted his disciples to see and live into, a world that would be blessed through him. His follower John would eventually understand. He wrote, "The Word became flesh and made his home among us. He was full of unfailing love and faithfulness" (John 1:14).

This is how every Master teaches his disciples. With reflexive muscle memory, the Master simply crafts, tends, keeps, or nurtures; smoothly, intently, without hesitation or fear. The Master knows the terrain. Jesus knew the world that often struck fear into the disciples. Breathless they would stand beside Jesus, even while Jesus stepped confidently into the broken world around him. In the same way that a master-beekeeper doesn't even consider the stings and venom, Jesus saw beyond the invective of his enemies. He saw the big picture of God's domain and knew how God was at work all around them. Jesus moved into the neighbourhood without fear and taught his disciples, and teaches us, to do the same.

In time, at the Master's side, we too may become the kind of people who step intently into the world God made and loves. Reflexively our eyes will turn to our neighbourhoods and our own hands will know the contours of the world before us. On that day we will no longer be breathless with fear but with beauty.

Keystone People

"...That is how I'll spend my short life. The only way I can prove my love is by scattering flowers and these flowers are every little sacrifice, every glance and word, and the doing of the least of actions for love."
– St. Therese of Lisieux[3]

Several years ago my wife and I spent time in France. We traveled to Juno Beach where my relatives fought in World War II to liberate a small town along the Normandy coast. Bayeux, France, has at its centre a beautiful cathedral. It is a wonder of architecture that still stands even through multiple wars and conflicts. I was astonished at how the relatively thin stone masonry could uphold vaulted arches over the centuries; Bayeux Cathedral is a feat of engineering. The secret of its longevity rests in the precise placement of a few simple stones. Above every arch and vaulted ceiling in the Bayeux Cathedral rests a keystone.

Keystones are essential to the integrity of the whole structure. They are not typically the most elaborate or decorated part of the building, but without them the cathedral would not be stable. Arches cannot be finished unless the keystone is in place, even though they may be small and bear surprisingly little weight themselves. Keystones are positioned in such a way as to allow the rest of the arch or vault to retain their shape and support the load, a technique that has allowed stonemasons to build some of the world's most awe-inspiring structures.

In ecosystems, biologists have identified keystones of a different kind. Keystone species are animals that may not be the most elaborate or celebrated, but they hold a vital role in their environment. They provide essential support in small ways that make a big difference, so much so that without them the system may not be self-sustaining. If particular keystone species were to disappear, hundreds of other species could not thrive. Beavers, for example, are a keystone species. They build structures that allow wetlands to form, creating an environment for thousands of other plants, insects, and animals to live well. Honey bees are also known as a keystone species. As pollinators, honey bees visit millions of flowers in a surprisingly large area around their beehive. This pollination plays a pivotal role in helping plants reproduce, grow fruit, and support other insects, birds, and humans. Yes, you and I rely on bees. More than one-third of all the food we eat is directly affected by the work of these pollinators. Keystone species, although not the most interesting or noteworthy from a distance, are essential in sustaining the whole through their minute and valuable work. We enjoy the food we eat and the beautiful world we live in thanks largely to very small, but precisely placed, creatures.

When I first learned that honey bees were a keystone species, I was intrigued. How could something so small, so apparently insignificant, be so pivotal and vital to the health of our world? I set up a bench outside my beehive and would watch as the honey bees would come and go, working day in and out visiting millions of flowers and trees in my neighbourhood. As my own imagination started to wrap itself around the enormity of the task that these honey bees engaged in, I was enthralled. Like little bottle-rockets, the honey bees start their day launching from the hive and return after pollinating thousands of plants. Their hard work makes my neighbourhood beautiful, and I barely see them working. It was not until I slowed down enough, sat among the flowers myself, and listened for the 'buzz' that I could see their minuscule efforts taking shape all around me. I knew the honey bee was responsible for much of the produce I buy at the grocery store, and I vaguely understood that they pollinate the hay that the cows eat, but to know that they were making the world around me come alive - I was awestruck.

Do I, as a pastor and neighbour, move about my neighbourhood slowly, attentively, patiently, and with a focus to bring life? Do I make things beautiful? Do I ensure that others benefit from the life I lead? Do I start my day intent on leaving it better than I found it? Do I work with others to find creative ways of helping my city thrive? I asked myself, "Am I a keystone person?"

Keystone people may not be the most noticeable or celebrated, but through their care and attentiveness they become essential to their neighbourhood. They support and give shape to the health of their community. Keystone neighbours are life-giving people who in time become so important to the world they help create. I wondered, if I moved away or was removed from my neighbourhood, would it be a sad day? Would people realize that something good, refreshing, and life-giving had left? I wondered...

Am I a keystone person?

This question is, in many ways, the foundation of this book. I questioned the impact of my life and faith as I watched those bees come and go from their hive. Was I merely working for my own benefit? I could say that I was working for the wellbeing of my closest friends and family, but was I truly tending to the betterment of my whole city in a lasting way? My experience at the beehive raised this very important question. Was I postured in such a way to bring life to the world around me, and what would need to change in my own imagination to become that kind of person?

Becoming a keystone person was, in my mind, different than becoming a 'pillar of the community.' These people are often seen and celebrated in neighbourhoods across the country, and they are vital. Active and involved community advocates are important, and those who love their neighbourhoods will actively seek ways to build important committees, institutions, churches, community leagues, businesses, better governance, and societies. As these organizations grow, they carry the weight of programs and projects that help cities operate and serve their people well.

Keystone people hold another function. They are are precisely placed, and work in often unseen ways, to hold the space before them. Keystone people are the community connectors, those who see small ideas and bring them to life. They are the eyes of the city, the sages who observe and find patterns. They work to bring pieces together, redeem what is broken, and strive for peace. Keystone people instill a sense of hope that grows beyond themselves, often sacrificially. They love deeply and genuinely, serving with a deep character-shaped influence. They are humble and create a culture of growth, breathing life into everything they do.

Elizabeth Sweetheart is a keystone person. She was raised in Nova Scotia, but now in her 70s lives in New York. She's known as the Green Lady of Brooklyn. Why? Because everything she has, wears, and does is connected to the colour green. Her hair is green, tucked back behind her green glasses, and the bright green colours she loves make her a beloved character in her neighbourhood.[4] But her quirky passion for the colour green has made her more than a passing novelty. She has found a way to live out her passion for the colour in an authentic way that has opened doors and made connections. One neighbour said, "I've been here for my entire life and if I didn't see her around here, I would definitely feel there's something missing."[5] Instead of saying Elizabeth Sweetheart is an outsider, her neighbours talk about how deeply they would miss her if she was gone. She brings pizzaz to the place she lives. Little do they know, a green-loving lady is a keystone that holds good things together in their neighbourhood.

We are often nervous about being a quirky neighbour; we might stick out just a bit too much, maybe seem pretentious. But it's not. Anyone can become a loving and uniquely authentic character in the story of their neighbourhood. When people see what's behind the mask, and enjoy all our passions, they come alive too. Elizabeth Sweetheart does not hold political clout in her city, but she has become life and joy to her neighbours. Who would have thought that a keystone person could be a woman decked out in the full neon spectrum of the colour green? Who could imagine that the keystone person in your neighbourhood may be you?

Another keystone person is David Young in New Orleans. After Hurricane Katrina, whole areas of New Orleans were abandoned and left to waste away. Grocery stores were wiped out and those who came back discovered that they did not have easy access to the food they needed. David Young decided to change the story of the Lower Ninth Ward by planting gardens and orchards for people to access fresh seasonal fruit. Something else happened that changed the way he sought to redeem this broken and damaged part of the world. Young realized that there was a need for pollinators to help his gardens thrive, so he eventually became a beekeeper and today manages about twenty beehives with his organization *Capstone* (visit capstone118.org). His honey is made available to the community at low cost, and the bees help his gardens to flourish. Today his team of volunteers have made this place thrive again. From wasteland to productive farmland, one man had played a pivotal role in bringing life and community together again. David Young is a keystone person.

Jesus was a keystone person. All around Jesus were religious leaders who were vying for their own glory, and political leaders who were struggling for power. But Jesus, this miracle-working-man, was not striving for either power or glory in the sense that the people of that day would expect. In time Jesus' disciples began to make sense, albeit in fits and starts, of what Jesus was doing among them. Jesus came to be near and to bring life. Jesus came to live with and among the people he loved. Not only to experience the daily grind of the fishmongers, but to show these fishermen the Father's heart - loving and redeeming his creation. This redemptive love pivoted not on a throne or through a media campaign. Jesus did not achieve his Father's purposes with a war or with a government. Rather, all that the Father completed in Jesus happened in the most well-placed, small, and beautiful acts of love and grace the world has ever known. Jesus was precisely where the Father wanted him to be, demonstrating this profound posture of grace and love.

Peter saw the poetry in it all. He saw the subversive and perfect way that Jesus worked to establish the Kingdom of God. In Acts 4, Peter is preaching and says, "For Jesus is the one referred to in the Scriptures, where it says, 'The stone that you builders rejected has now become the cornerstone.' There is salvation in no one else!" (Acts 4:11-12). Peter is saying that Jesus is the keystone, the pivotal piece that holds everything together. By the world's standards, Jesus should have been in the reject pile - an inefficient ruler, a weak warrior, and a soft politician. He was not the pillar of glory and power that the world would expect from the Almighty-God-become-man. But the One who was rejected became the Saviour of the whole, who through love, sacrifice, and obedience, became the Keystone upon which the Kingdom of God is built.

If Jesus became the keystone, then could we be invited to be his keystone people? Are we standing in-between to bless, uphold, and love those around us? Does the life of Jesus serve as a central point of reference for how we bring life to our neighbourhood? The answer to these questions could change the whole shape of our lives. As keystone people, in the way of Jesus, we become those who stand in the gap, serve the whole, and live lives that reflect Jesus' posture of love. Yet even those who followed Jesus did not become keystone people who perfectly reflected the kind of life that Jesus lived. They could not clearly see the big picture of God's love for the people God made or the world God created. Something had to happen in their imaginations and hearts before they could become the kind of people that God was shaping them to be. Before they could love, they needed to be taught an important lesson about their own identities. The earliest followers of Jesus had to be reminded first and foremost that they were, themselves, beloved. Before God could call the world to love its neighbours, it needed to see how deep and wide was God's love for them.

Loved

"He is doing this life with me;
Completely and uniquely living my experience.
Love has gone this far."
- John Lynch[6]

Who you are matters. This whole conversation begins here. Our identity will shape the way we step into the world around us. When I sit down in the mornings to read and pray, my bookmark is a little piece of paper that falls onto my lap. It's a basic reminder of who I am. It says, "You belong to the Father, Son and Spirit. You always have. You always will. He loves you and likes you. You are his beloved child." This is food for my soul. It is the fuel of identity that moves me into my day. I need to hear this before I turn to my neighbour and before I connect with others. I need to know what is true about me because what is true about me is also true about everyone I will encounter.

From the very start, and even before the very start, God has delighted in you. You are not incidental to God. When God was creating and pondering who should be created, God thought about and made a way for... you. He loves, and likes, the 'you' sitting right where you are. Even now, God thinks the world of you. God sees someone we look at, but don't see. God sees someone deeply loved. God sees you as he sees his son, Jesus.

Even at your most awful, you are so much more than you feel you may be. John Lynch wrote that on your worst day, you are, get this:

"Adored, enjoyed, clean, righteous, absolutely forgiven, new, acceptable, complete, chosen, able, intimately loved, smiled upon, planned for, protected, continually thought about, enjoyed, cared for, comforted, understood, known completely, given all mercy, compassion, guarded, matured, bragged on, defended, valued, esteemed, held, hugged and caressed, kissed, heard, honored, in unity with, favored, enough, on time, lacking nothing, directed, guided continually, never failed, waited for, anticipated, part of, belonging, never alone, praised, secure, safe, believed, appreciated, given all grace, all patience, at peace with, pure, shining, precious, cried over, grieved with, strengthened, emboldened, drawn kindly to repentance, relaxed with, never on trial, never frowned at, never hit with a two-by-four, at rest in, receiving complete access, given gifts, given dreams, given new dreams, continually healed, nurtured, carried, never mocked, never punished, most of my humor enjoyed, not behind, not outside, given endless affection."[7]

I love John Lynch's list. It is profound. But truthfully, I barely believe most of it. Most days I look in the mirror at a guy who can be defensive, yet here I learn that God sees me as one who is defended. I look at a man who is nervous, yet God sees the bold courage of Jesus in me. I think others look at me and see my imprudence or my inability. Through Jesus, God sees that I am fully welcomed in, made whole and able. This list is almost surreal, as though God truly looks through, past, or around the reality we look at in that bathroom mirror. We judge what we look at and say that God is just blind to accept a bunch of obvious failures or pompous posers into God's inner circle. Maybe so, but there is more to the story.

Our identity, in God's eyes, centres around Jesus. Like a perfect robe covering filthy clothes, Jesus embraces us and makes us glow with his radiance; we are reminded that we are made in the image of God and seen entirely anew. No matter what we think about what we look at in the mirror, the truth of who we are is forever and inextricably changed because of Jesus. This reality changes what God sees when God looks at us. On your worst day you are perfectly loved in God's eyes because of Jesus. Perhaps this list is true. Perhaps the way we have been looking at ourselves is not at all the way that God has been looking at us. Perhaps God has, from the beginning, been so delighted in who you are that he is holding you in his gaze, laughing and celebrating every small moment that you discover what God has known about you from the start. You are more loved and more delighted in than you know.

Here is something more. God sees you in a way that is so profoundly beautiful and liberating that when we start to catch glimpses of it ourselves, we start down a road we could never have known existed. This beloved creation of God discovers something stunning. The One who first helped you 'see' that you are his beloved creation, now helps you 'see' that those around you were made by the same hands. Because of Jesus, everyone you meet, everyone who looks at themselves blindly, is beautiful and beloved. All that is impossibly and wonderfully true about you on your worst day is also true of those who live on your street. This is the great news of Jesus for you and for them.

There is icing on this cake. Not only are you deeply beloved and tenderly gifted and made whole before God, and not only does God profoundly delight in every person you meet, but you get to be a part of making all that is beautiful to God a reality to the people in the place where you live. You are part of what God is doing. The God who created you has made you a co-creator with the Maker of Life.

And in God's eyes, on your worst day, you're already fit to start making something beautiful.

The Smallest of the Birds

"Symbols are earth's windows to heaven: they are islands in the cosmos where human vision assumes a curious double focus, perceiving now a piece of creation, now a flash of the Creator's deeper, vaster world beyond."
-Markus Bockmehl[8]

For thousands of years, honey bees have played a small but beautiful role in helping people follow God into the places where they live. From the biblical promised land of "milk and honey" to medieval spiritual writing and even Christian architecture, the thematic thread of honey bees has had an impact on how people live in and bless the world around them. As I quietly explored my own apiary I found that I was being led on a journey into my neighbourhood. That journey led to a discovery that I did not expect. I was not alone. Many have gone before me, moving from the apiary and finding that God was leading them into the places where they lived. God is making all things new, and we are being invited to participate in this life-giving, redemptive work.

Nine hundred years ago people like us also sat in front of beehives and wondered about what God was teaching them about the world around them. Reflecting on the natural environment became such a spiritual experience that medieval Christians wrote books about their observations called 'bestiaries.' Bestiaries are a fascinating glimpse into the medieval age of allegory, natural history, and spiritual formation. Part science text, with hand-drawn illustrations of both common and exotic animals, and part devotional text with lessons for life and faith, the medieval bestiary is an invitation into a strange, mystical, and more than slightly inaccurate world. A medieval bestiary of 1187 describes the fox, for example, as a "crafty and deceitful animal that never runs in a straight line, but only in circles."[9] Or of apes, "...said to be ugly, dirty beasts with flat and wrinkled noses; their rear parts are particularly horrible." These not-quite-so-scientific observations about animals (and sometimes rocks and mermaids) were collected together to play another important role. They were meant to serve as spiritual or moral guidebooks. To some medieval minds the natural world was a rich mine of wisdom, and every aspect of it pointed in some way to knowing God and God's purposes for us. The world could be 'read' and each plant, cat, bird, and elephant had some attribute that awakened a sense of God's glory. Markus Bockmuehl wrote that for Christians of that era, "the world was abrim with such pointers to God and to spiritual truth."[10] The bestiary reminded Christians of important moral lessons, or deeper still, of God's supreme design for each creature and each life. Medieval priests could turn to bestiaries - rich compendia full of creative sermon illustrations and spiritual lessons, and share these insight with their church community. To anyone listening about how the fox is like the devil, sneaky and crafty, it would have seemed as though the whole world was created to tell a story. With each animal, from goat to bee, pointing to Christ, the natural world became a living, breathing, proclamation of God's tender love. Anyone, literate or not, could deepen their devotion and draw closer to God simply by observing the world around them.

Honey bees have a particularly interesting and noteworthy description in the medieval bestiaries. In one fifteenth-century hand-written manuscript called *The Bestiary of Anne Walshe*,[11] there is a fascinating description of honey bees: "Bees are the smallest of birds. They are born from the bodies of oxen, or from the decaying flesh of slaughtered calves; worms form in the flesh and then turn into bees. Bees live in community, choose the most noble among them as king, have wars, and make honey. Their laws are based on custom, but the king does not enforce the law; rather the lawbreakers punish themselves by stinging themselves to death. Bees are afraid of smoke and are excited by noise. Each has its own duty: guarding the food supply, watching for rain, collecting dew to make honey, and making wax from flowers."[12]

Although mostly inaccurate in light of today's understanding of honey bees, this brief description is still richly descriptive of what people would have seen: foraging bees working together to maintain order and productivity. Honey bees were very much respected by these medieval authors as noble, hardworking, and selfless. As unscientific as this 900-year-old description may be for us today, the deep sense of wonder that honey bees inspired was no less real. Insects that created honey and wax, while causing no harm to fruit and serving their king (queen) faithfully as a united community - it was perfect fuel for spiritual reflection.

Yet for all their mistaken descriptions of bees, and the diverse spiritual lessons they drew from their observations, these medieval Christians found a way to posture their lives towards learning from the world around them. In each animal they could find something instructive, inspiring, and heartfelt. Their enthusiasm for welcoming God into the daily rhythm of their lives is a beautiful outcome of their belief that God was present and working in their midst. Embracing the small and subtle, as well as the wild and untamed, led them to adore and delight in God and God's world.

Throughout the centuries, others have also been mesmerized and personally shaped by observing honey bees. Later in his life the great Russian author Leo Tolstoy sought, almost simultaneously, a life of faith and a passion for beekeeping. In fact his wife, Sonja, wrote in her diary that Tolstoy was so enamoured with honey bees, that "The apiary has become the centre of his world for him now, and everyone has to be interested in bees!"[13] As his passion for honey bees grew so did his love for others. Tolstoy, who was known as being a hard and driven man, was shaped by his time in the apiary. Throughout his book *War and Peace*, Tolstoy used his experiences as a beekeeper to reflect on the human condition. The sweet gentle buzz of honey bees have a way of drawing attention to the world around us and, like Tolstoy, honey bees help us return to our senses. The warmth of a summer apiary invites our focus to centre in on the nuanced beauty of those blossoms by our feet and our own relationship to simple life found all around. To consider that God has, perpetually, the smallest creatures in his purview should give us a Tolstoylian double-take when we consider our relationship to those creatures made in God's image - namely, the people living next door.

My own faith journey has led me to a love for the natural world of bees and flowers. I now leap up from my chair and run over to catch a glimpse of a bee-fly dart across the yard. I settle in nice and close when my honey bees are fanning the late afternoon heat at the entrance of their hive. The full majesty of little insects almost consumes me when I draw near to their world. Unlike the medieval bestiaries, I do not construct far-fetched allegories from observing my bees, and I do prefer the more accurate modern-day descriptions of honey bees and their behaviour. But my awe over these small workers and their beautiful community is burgeoning. In fact, honey bees are changing my posture towards the world I live in. The way I see the world is being renewed through a small lens and at a slower pace. My curious fascination at the hive entrance has not left me sitting there. I am surprised to find that as a result I am increasingly curious and astonished by the people who live along the street I call home.

Beekeeping has made me perk up to the fact that creatures far more amazing and beautiful shuffle by me everyday. Kids on their wobbly training wheels, teachers herding in a classroom after recess, or a grandparent counting off nickels and quarters in the grocery store line ahead of me. They are all amazing. I even see the guy tailgating me on the highway a little bit differently, not as the jerk we might think him to be, but as the beloved person God created to join with God in making all things new. Those who have been stung by a honey bee will, in a moment, see nothing but a wicked little insect. Yet for all the stings I've received over the years (mind you, it has been very few), I have spent enough time observing the beautiful capacity of these bees that their stings make up only one small part of what makes them uniquely beautiful. Like the angry person in the big truck blazing past me on the highway, I'm starting to put even his failure into perspective. Honey bees and the world we live in us teach us some vital lessons about what God is up to.

Bees have become, for me and countless before me, a symbol of something more. I have come to reject the idea that the world around me has nothing to say about God, about humanity, or about my posture towards both. In a world where we often strip down anything beautiful to its most basic functions, we often miss the glowing chorus of voices pointing to something more, something deeper, and something that stretches our imaginations beyond what we know. Through my time in the apiary I have learned to allow the bees to show me, whether literally or symbolically, the beauty of God's work all around me.

It is God's world after all. Are we open to allowing God the pleasure of showing it to us through his eyes?

Promised Land

"We come from the earth, we return to the earth, and in between we garden."
-Author Unknown

The overarching story of God in the Bible is one of redemption. God is mending what is broken, finding what was lost, embracing the unloved, and bringing life to parched land. The whole story is one where God is really bringing the whole world back into right relationship with himself. It is a love story where we soon find that we are characters in the surprising and unfolding narrative. We have a part to play. In reading and engaging the story of God, we are brought to a point, a crux, where we have to wonder, "Am I participating in the redemption of this world, too? Or am I just an observer while God and others bring life and beauty to the places and in the community where I live?"

Certain images in the Bible reveal the hope of God for the broken world, and offer an entry point for our participation with God in making all things new. One theme is the garden. From the first moments in the Garden of Eden, to the last book of the Bible, there is a green vein that runs throughout the scriptures. God is planting life, and is inviting us to be a part of the redemption of all things.

The biblical text often reveals the story of God through the touchable realities of the land in which God was at work. Through a talking donkey, a shady tree, or a flowing river, the land of the Bible provides a detailed backdrop for God's story of redemption and love. The land that God promised to God's people was often referred to as the land of milk and honey, a place of life and hope where families could settle and enjoy their own gardens. The picture of peace was green, alive, and gave hope that God would truly bring about a final redemption of all things. This imagery of a land of milk and honey was a concept that oozed with hope and the dreams of those who yearned for God's goodness again.

Yet even as recently as 20 years ago when I first visited Israel, there was little evidence of honey in ancient Israel. Everywhere people looked, beekeeping did not seem to be in the archaeological record. Although the Bible is full of references to honey, biblical scholars began to assume that this meant date honey, not bee honey. Then, in 2007, archaeologists made a fascinating discovery.[14] In a once densely populated part of the ancient city of Rehov, Israel, they found the remnants of a large apiary, about 100 clay beehives believed to be about 3,000 years old. Some archaeologists suspect that the bees were kept in the dense urban area to protect their valuable asset. They wondered if perhaps bees on a hillside would be threatened by wild animals or raiders, and they said that it is puzzling to find so many beehives in the middle of a city. Honey bees, it turns out, were an important part of urban and agricultural life - a rich source of sweet goodness. They found that this was indeed a land flowing with milk and real bee honey, right in the middle of a city.

It's in this context of urban beekeeping that the Old Testament first refers to the Promised Land as the land of milk and honey. In fact, before the people of Israel entered the land of Canaan, they sent in a team of spies to scout out the land, to look for trees, fertile soil, and crops. What they found was life! Numbers 13 recounts how the spies found clusters of grapes so big that it took two men to carry them. They found pomegranates and figs and reported back to Moses saying, "We entered the land you sent us to explore, and it is indeed a bountiful country - a land flowing with milk and honey" (Numbers 13:27). With luscious fruit and fertile land, there is no wonder that it would be flowing with honey. The bees were busy and the people benefited from their hard work. Both honey and milk are harvested resources, and harvesting implies settled times of peace and prosperity. God's promised land was a land where people could put down roots, enjoy raising a family, care for their livestock, and gather honey from their bees. It was a strong picture that would have made mouths water, not just for the produce, but for the promise of dwelling together in safety. The story of God's care for his people involved the provision of land as a place to settle and celebrate God's faithfulness. Honey was a symbol of rest and hope, something the people of God desperately longed for after centuries of slavery and decades of wandering in the wilderness. It was a profoundly redemptive image.

Today many of our neighbourhoods are pollinator dead-zones. New developments have a sterile way of reintroducing green space. The once rich biodiversity of weeds, grass, forests, ponds, and shrubs are replaced with sidewalks, turf, and a row of trees. We replace soil in playgrounds with safety rubber from old tires and trees with bright yellow monkey bars. Front yards are home to driveways, not gardens, and those beneficial insects which do find their way into our neighbourhoods find no logs to move into. In reality most are chased off by a can of Raid. This sterility is not a picture of the land of milk and honey but of wilderness. Wilderness is for wandering, not for establishing a home. When we plant gardens and give homes to honey bees, even in our urban or suburban landscapes, we become those who remember and delight in the Promised Land of God. In many neighbourhoods there are those who come and go and don't care about the soil or the trees, but God's people bring fertility back to the land. They hopefully long for the Promised Land with a bag full of tulip bulbs, a pile of compost, and a buzzing beehive.

Many cities are starting to change. The urban beekeeping movement is taking root and even cities like New York are experiencing a resurgence of urban gardening and beekeeping. Rooftops and backyard patios are once again alive with the same sense of abundance that made the Promised Land so alluring and hopeful thousands of years ago.

When we first moved to Chestermere, the city had bylaws against keeping honey bees in gardens. I enjoyed honey bees and loved what they brought to my yard and neighbourhood. So we began a conversation about bringing back the bees. I spoke to nearly 1,000 kids in the local schools and pre-schools about honey bees. We started the Chestermere Honey Bee Society, and bit by bit we changed the perceptions people had about honey bees. Kids were the first to notice the absence of bees in their gardens and got their parents to plant more flowers. A group of grade one kids wrote letters to the mayor, and soon city council agreed: we need bees.

In the summer of 2016 Chestermere became the first city in Western Canada to become a certified "Bee City." It was a very big deal. In her letter of acceptance to our city, Gillian Leitch, the Program Director of Bee City Canada wrote, "Thank you so much for the work you have already done to champion pollinators in your place and for mentoring this love and beauty to the rest of Canada." What began as a dream to turn my yard from a gravel patch into a green space has become a community effort to make our whole city a beautiful place to live - and now we are part of a national conversation. It is inspiring to think that community groups, schools, gardeners, and business owners are working together to find ways to ensure that our city is green, lush, and buzzing with life. In a few short years the community rallied to move our city from a pollinator dead zone, to a bee-friendly, garden-celebrating municipality. When people come together and work for the betterment of their city, good things happen. It may not yet be the land of milk and honey, but keystone people are making our city a land with much promise. The sound of bees is the sound of redeemed land and thriving neighbourhoods.

In the biblical story, God's picture of renewal and redemption was connected to this sense of bringing life back to the land. God's people longed for a land where everyone could have gardens, flocks, and honey bees. This 'milk and honey' imagery, rich with cultural meaning, was not lost on Jesus. Not only was Jesus bringing healing, forgiveness, and hope to this people, pressured as they were by high taxes and Roman oppression, he was reminding people of God's redemptive move to bring life to the people and the land again. Not only for the Jews in the land of Israel, but to the whole world: from Jerusalem to Chestermere. In fact, some texts hint at the kind of hopeful message Jesus was giving when he spoke to his disciples. When Jesus met the disciples after the resurrection, they ate broiled fish, and in the Aramaic version of the text, he also ate honeycomb (Luke 24:42). Jesus spoke Aramaic and so it may have been meaningful to the first Aramaic-speaking Christians to highlight this particular detail - that Jesus was bringing back life to their homeland. God's power to resurrect Jesus affirms the ancient promises given by God to his people, to provide a safe place for them. Here we see the resurrected Jesus eating honey in the land of milk and honey - a compelling image of God's continued faithfulness and redemptive work in the Promised Land.

Yet even without this interesting parallel at the end of Luke, we see throughout Scripture the story of God's ongoing attention to the places, locations, and activities of God's people. God is interested in blessing the land and giving life to God's people. The land of milk and honey was truly intended to be a place where the alien and foreigner are safe, where the poor are cared for, where debts are forgiven, and where God's people reflect the redemptive heart of God. Your balcony or front yard is a sign of God's redemptive and hope-filled work in your midst today. The food you share with your neighbours says what you believe about the hope you have. We are co-creators with God in making the places where we live a foretaste of God's dream for this world. What is your table saying about the resources God has blessed you with? What is your garden saying about the land God has give to you?

Bees in the Belfry

Honey bees were an important part of neighbourhood life in medieval Scotland. In those days honey bees were housed in skeps, woven basket-like beehives made of straw. These traditional skeps did not stand up to weather very well, and so small alcoves were built into the walls of castles, houses, and monasteries throughout the country and even across Europe. Beekeepers in Scottish towns and villages would place their skeps in these alcoves, also known as bee-boles, to protect them. Today historians have made connections between these bee-boles and the local parish. They have found that honey was a valuable commodity given as rent or tithe to the church, while the beeswax was used to make candles. It made sense to keep bees.

Although medieval Europe held bees in high esteem, commending them for their nobility among God's creatures, their production of honey and wax made them a practical and utilitarian asset. It was not until the nineteenth century that the pollination of plants was first understood scientifically, and only later still did scientists come to appreciate and value the importance of honey bees for pollinating and beautifying fields and gardens.

So it was a surprising discovery when, in 2010, architects working on the 600-year-old Rosslyn Chapel in Scotland came across beehives, but not like any they had seen before. These hives were not in accessible alcoves built into the walls of the church for gathering wax and honey. Rather they were found high up in the pinnacles of the structure, completely inaccessible and largely unknown to the church. BBC News reported the discovery as a mystery.[15] They found that the ancient stone pinnacles were built with a little flower-shaped hole carved into them where bees could enter and create their hive. Inside each stone pinnacle were the perfectly preserved remains of bee colonies. Presumably hundreds of generations of honey bees used these hives and pollinated the surrounding parish for centuries. Rosslyn Chapel staff captured the discovery this way: "When the chapel was built, bees were considered to be sacred creatures, known as 'small messengers of God'. The hives at the chapel were never intended to be a source of honey but simply protective havens for the craftsmen's sacred friends, the bees."[16]

I contacted Malcolm Mitchell, the project architect who was working on the conservation of Rosslyn Chapel at the time of the discovery. I asked him to offer his thoughts about the discovery. In an email he said, "As the honey could not be harvested I believe that they provided the hives as an act of kindness...I'm sure that the clergy will have kept bees for harvesting honey and wax elsewhere and they would have understood that the actions of the bees were an intrinsic part of the well being of nature." The honey bees, it would seem, were intentionally accommodated by the forward-thinking church, or at the very least a creative team of church architects and stonemasons.

It's enticing to think that Rosslyn Chapel was built in part to bless the neighbourhood. That the builders understood the importance of honey bees and provided space for beehives strikes me as a deeply benevolent gesture. Whether they did so purely for the bees, or understood the beauty that bees brought to a surrounding community, is still a point of conjecture. The renovations were completed and Rosslyn Chapel was modernized. But the architects decided to keep the mysterious beehives with the hope that the bees could return and once again bring life to the neighbourhood around Rosslyn Chapel. Then, in June 2015, the Chapel reported that bees had, in fact, returned. Once again Rosslyn Chapel was a home to these "sacred friends,"[17] and once again this chapel played a vital role in bringing life to gardens and flowering fields across their parish. It is a beautiful image.

Imagine if the Church today took the same posture towards their neighbourhood as Rosslyn Chapel took 600 years ago and again today. That God's people, rooted in particular neighbourhoods, would recognize the role they play to bless the places where they live. Imagine if churches had that kind of small, bee-sized vision for making neighbourhoods lush and fruitful, or that long-term vision to realize that generation after generation will benefit from their creativity. Or imagine their humility to build these small beehives, hidden as they were, away from the celebratory spotlight. These beehives were marked with nothing but a little carved flower so high up that few knew that they existed. Yet every flower and fruit-bearing tree for miles around was given life because of their presence.

In some ways, the posture of those fifteenth-century church builders reminds me of Saint Thérèse of Lisieux who likened herself to a little flower - small and beloved. Saint Thérèse believed that the smallness of flowers allowed for God's glory to shine through. She said, "By stooping down to them, He manifests His infinite grandeur. The sun shines equally both on cedars and on every tiny flower. In just the same way God looks after every soul as if it had no equal. All is planned for the good of every soul, exactly as the seasons are so arranged that the humblest daisy blossoms at the appointed time."[18] Whether we are creating grand chapels or serving in simple ways, directing our creativity and efforts towards blessing the neighbourhood around us in small, unseen, and beautiful ways, with a view to the long term, is truly a reflection of God's work in our midst. What does it look like for churches today to build modern-day 'beehives'? What are those small, unseen, and deeply impacting actions that transform, beautify, and redeem the people and places around us? We are being called to become those people who bless far and wide, living out our love and faith in the spirit of those who first built Rosslyn Chapel with a buzzing vision for lush verdant life all around.

Beekeepers-Back

History provides inspiration for seeing our neighbourhood anew. But we do not have to be historians to discover how beekeeping leads us into the neighbourhood. The very act of beekeeping, including the tedious tasks, sticky messes, and itchy bee stings, have been helpful for me as I reflect on how I am being shaped to love others well. We often snap pictures of honey bees on flowers and eagerly hand out gifts of glistening jars full with golden honey. Every beekeeper will sit long and tell stories about how amazing honey bees are and how important they are to our world and wellbeing. Yet most beekeeping is less than extraordinary, and yet that makes it no less meaningful in preparing our hearts to move into the places where God is at work among us. In fact it may be in these less glamorous moments that we learn the most.

Have you heard of 'beekeepers-back'? I hadn't until I started to lift heavy honey-supers (the parts of the beehive that weigh about 40 pounds when full of honey). When I met life-long beekeepers with broken backs, I knew it was a hazard of the profession. 'Beekeepers-back' is a real thing. How about I add a few more terms from my beekeeping experience. I have learned first-hand about 'I-didn't-know-bees-can-sting-through-my-bee-suit' and 'It's-smoking-hot-out-here-why-am-I-wearing-head-to-toe-coveralls-and-starting-a-fire-for-my-bee-smoker-I-must-be-crazy.' These, I'm certain, are real terms used by beekeepers everywhere.

For all the idealistic beauty and grace of honey bees, the experience of keeping bees can sometimes be un-extraordinary or mildly chaotic. From cleaning old brood boxes to agonizing over a queen-less hive, there are messy realities to beekeeping. I will often get calls from beekeeping hopefuls who have heard about the problems with honey bees and want to help by having a hive for themselves. Invariably the well-intentioned caller will ask, "How easy is it and how much time do I have to put in?" or worse still, "How much honey can I get?" For some, honey bees are not viewed through the important lens of animal husbandry. They are not seen as creatures we care for, season after season, for the wellbeing of our neighbourhoods. These interested callers see honey bees as a means to an end, and that end often looks like a jar of honey. Idealistic visions of beekeeping will not save the bees, but 'beekeepers-back' will.

Here's how Dan White Jr. wrote about the challenge of idealism today: "Idealism in its culturally appropriated forms infects our ability to accept reality, work within reality and find real contentment within reality. Idealism has infiltrated most of our society and cajoles us to exalt our preferred dreams as authority over the raw, complicated, messy, relational material before us."[19] The reality of beekeeping is mostly messy, mostly sweaty, and sometimes painful. On honey-extraction day everything in the house and garage becomes a sticky mess, the floors and door knobs become ready reminders of my work. Farmers, parents, and gardeners soon realize that idealism will not create growth. There is more to raising a child than cuddles, and there is more to gardening than flowers. Whenever we enter into creating beauty and life with our eye only on the fruit we expect to harvest, we miss something much more profound.

Idealism distorts our focus and disorients our direction. Like those who only see the beehive for the honey, we are at a loss when idealism drives our expectations. Beekeeping has tempered my idealism and opened my eyes to see people around me anew. If I expected my neighbour to be Mr. Rogers and my home to be a beacon of Martha Stewart-like hospitality, I will be sadly disappointed when I discover that my neighbour is painfully shy or my home looks more like the grand finale of a kindergarten convention. The raw, messy, and relational material of our homes and neighbourhood are the real stuff of goodness and beauty. Our idealism may be shattered when we discover that all is not healthy or well on our street, in our homes, or in our churches. Yet when we lay down our idealistic visions and stop chasing after the end-result we've envisioned for our neighbourhood, we begin to see something emerge that can transform how we live and thrive.

As a beekeeper, I am an environmentalist. I'm interested in creating a safe place, an environment, for my honey bees to thrive. I don't know if they'll produce honey, and I don't know if they'll make it through the winter. Through my sweat and aching back, I set about to help or intervene when a disease wreaks havoc, but at other key times I let them work through their challenges themselves. Through it all I offer the best possible environment and conditions for life. When failure comes, I recognize that it is part of the journey and make plans for the next season.

It has been said that if beekeepers ever say that they know what they are doing, don't trust a word of it. At our very core, beekeepers barely manage controlled chaos. One season I had a hive with some problems, and the solution was to shake out all 20,000 bees onto my grass. My neighbours must have thought I was out of my mind, standing there in my full beekeepers suit, bees and honey and hive equipment strewn across my yard. If they thought I was nuts, I felt all the more so. From catching bee swarms in thick bush or under a deck, to unwrapping a beehive after a long, cold winter, beekeepers can only engage the space where the bees live. We cannot direct them, contain them, or order them about. Yet for all that we are unable to do, creating healthy space for the bees is often all that is needed for them to thrive. The bees I shook out on my lawn found their way into the hive and reorganized themselves (becoming my very best hive, I should add). And the swarm we found under the deck is happily living on an acreage. Honey bees are among the oldest 'domesticated' animals that have been tended to for millennia. And yet no beekeeper can ever predict what any single honey bee will do. Wild and unconfined, honey bees teach us the beauty and sweetness of a life that is not governed by idealistic expectations and demands.

We take the same approach with our neighbourhoods and communities. We are not sure if they will thrive or produce. We may not know if they will love well, become places of hope and beacons of beauty and goodness. Our role is to create an environment for life and trust to grow. When we put the weight of our idealism aside and when we file away our expectations, we experience raw, relational, and complex beauty that lifts up our gaze to 'see' others in new and fresh ways. We begin to see the people around us with a gracious love that demands nothing and seeds hope in everything. We become keystone people, learning to live among others in the Jesus Way. Putting our backs into it.

How we 'put our backs into it,' however, is not through a list of techniques or systems. That's definitely not what this book is about. It is through a renewed vision of God's work in our hearts, our imaginations, and our neighbourhoods. It is here, as people with a growing grasp of God's love for us, that we begin the journey. We turn and posture our lives to make visible the invisible beauty all around us.

Part Two:

Making the Invisible Visible

"...and Revery"

Beekeeping is an attentive exercise. In times past, beekeepers would spend their days at the hive entrance, watching, listening, and learning from the bees. Heinrich Storch's book, *At the Hive Entrance*, was for me a valuable handbook for observing what was happening inside the hive, just by watching the bees coming and going. Storch was of the firm belief that honey bees should not be disturbed often, and that beekeepers were at their best when they allowed bees to be bees, intervening only when they saw the need. He said, "As long as the beekeeper cannot understand the internal condition of the hive by watching the outside, he can only lose money and will have to pay his apprenticeship dearly."[20]

Part two of this book is an invitation to see, with new eyes, what is happening in the invisible places of our hearts and imaginations as we hope to become people who love our neighbourhoods well. I call it, "making the invisible visible." In my time sitting at the hive entrance, with bees zipping by me on their way to the gardens of my neighbourhood, I began to reflect on my own journey into the neighbourhood. I found that my own eyes were being opened to see my heart and neighbours anew.

The six chapters in the second part of this book seek to capture the postures and practices that I have adopted as a pastor and beekeeper entering into my own neighbourhood. They are:

-Beauty: The breath of fresh air that awakens us to see, feel, and engage again.
-Awe: Choosing to allow the people we meet to trigger awe in the deep corners of our imaginations.
-Security: Re-envisioning what true safety means.
-Boring: Finding peace in the rhythms of neighbourhood life.
-Taste of Place: Your neighbourhood is unique in all the world
-Curates: We are the caregivers, shaping the culture of our neighbourhoods

In the following chapters we will explore these six postures and explore how our imaginations may be shaped anew. Beginning with a discovery of the beauty of God at work all around us and alive to participating in what God is doing, these simple postures will help us reflect on the next steps of this journey. They serve to reveal the existing patterns of our lives and the open door before us. They call us to step into practices that fuel and inspire the journey into our neighbourhoods and to discover the joy of God's Spirit at work in our midst, even now. These postures are not a how-to guide for being a better neighbour, although they might lead you there. Rather they position our imaginations, the stories and pictures that shape the way we see, to respond to the people and places where God has called us.

Emily Dickinson's poem, "To make a prairie" written in 1755 captures the essence of what it means to shape our imaginations and hearts to engage our neighbourhoods and to create something beautiful in the places where we live. She writes:

To make a prairie it takes a clover and one bee,
One clover, and a bee,
And revery.
The revery alone will do,
If bees are few.[21]

Her poem starts with this tender idea that one flower and one bee may create all that is beautiful. But then she pauses. No, there is more that is needed. In fact, maybe there is only one thing that is needed. More than the flower and the bee, we need revery. We need a dream. We need an imagination that wonders and delights in possibility. We need to begin here, and the very little we have - be it a flower or a bee, will be enough.

To shape our hearts to see the invisible beauty sprouting in our neighbourhoods and to become people who see the possibility of new life in the places where we live, we begin with a posture of renewed imagination for beauty. We begin with revery.

Awakening Beauty

Nocturne in E Flat Major

My mind was a cream soup of muddled thoughts as I drove east into the southern Alberta night. The highway was open and I had settled into that place where it's easy, and almost satisfying, to brood. Memories mixed with ideas and prayers. Words and feelings congealed into that kind of opaque directionless place where our minds sometimes go. We seldom talk about it. Maybe we cannot easily name it. Maybe it's just the place where we work things out; that ever-present puddle of thoughts that settles and stirs at the edge of our minds.

I had set the cruise control and set my own mind and heart in place; my thoughts moved to the same low rumble and sway of the aging Ford SUV. The headlights shone down the long road, but in my mind there was no halogen bulb lighting the way, just those familiar mixed textures of half-feelings and passing thoughts. Speaking with God is not easy here. A few words, a safe greeting, and a moment of silence to listen. It does not work. The soup and the rumble and the words fill the space and we were cut short. Guess I am not praying tonight. Sorry, Jesus.

It was cold and although the heater was turned up, my toes were stiff. I turned on the radio and in a moment the cab suddenly filled with piano music. Beautiful piano music. Perfect piano music. Simple and elegant, emotional and complex. Some late night radio show was playing Chopin's *Nocturne in E Flat Major*. And like some kind of gift, the music carried me and moved me. Rescued me. Calmed me. Gave me words. Not more words to add to the jumble, but fresh words that brought peace. Life. The dancing notes were like pegs on a wall, each a hanger where I could place my thoughts. Each chord an invitation forward. I could see, and I followed.

My imagination came to life. I could not only sense God's presence again, but felt as though Jesus was sitting right beside me, or behind me, or somehow on my own seat with me. Jesus was there all around and all along, his presence made clear as the music poured and danced through the musty car. The piano music washed away more than just the silence. I may have even laughed when, for this beautiful moment, the cloud of unknowing that was thick in my imagination suddenly and refreshingly evaporated to reveal Jesus. He was with me. Each note was somehow received by Jesus. Each one an invitation to speak to him. So I did. What started as giving turned into receiving and soon we were talking. Jesus and me, clear and safe, beautiful and full. The Lover and the beloved flying down the road into the darkness. But there was light.

Cataracts

"As we live with new eyes, we are astounded by the beauty of what we hold in our hearts, no less than the glory of God waiting to be expressed through human frailty."
- Mandy Smith[22]

We strain to see God's world through our cataract-dimmed eyes. When we are restricted in our ability to see or sense God we begin a rocky journey into ourselves, into a kind of closure. When we are blind to God, unable to see God's work in our lives or around us, we grow into a forgetful stasis. Out of sight and out of mind, as they say. We forget our identity in Christ, and we forget God's redemptive work in the world around us. We forget the love of the Father. Forgetfulness is painful because it leads us towards two insidious and damaging responses: fear and disbelief. The two are closely connected because when we live in fear, feeling apart from God's embrace, we cannot trust God's goodness towards us. When the Father is not someone we feel we can trust, we assume a posture of disbelief and fearful doubt.

In those moments where we cannot see God, when we imagine a false picture of the Father in our hearts, we react. We feel as though we are no longer sons and daughters, but orphans on the run. Adam and Eve had this move figured out. They ran, covered themselves, and hid. Without a clear vision of God-with-us and a sense of the Sprit working around us, we retract and close up. The pain, guilt and loneliness become too much for us. We cannot carry it, so we cover ourselves as best as we can. We busy ourselves with work and shallow pursuits, and we set our imaginations running after anything that will ease the pain. And those who simply do not have the energy, well, they give up. As apathy and fatalism set in many people simply become numb to life and to their neighbour. They cannot see who they are, who God is, and those who live around them. The strangest part is that we can do this all with a contrived smile, thinking, "This is just how things go." All the while life piles up around us. It's an ensnaring vortex that starts when our eyes are closed.

When we cannot see;
We forget, then;
We clam up with fear and disbelief, then;
We run, then;
We hide and cover up, then;
We put on a pained-fake grin and close our eyes some more.

The whole cycle begins by how we see the world around us. 'Seeing' is vital to our life and participation in the world-blessing work of God. Seeing enables us to imagine others, neighbours, co-workers, and grocery store clerks as the context through which everything that is good comes to life. The lonely older man down the street, the couple with three children next door, or the teenagers who ride their bikes across our lawns are all part of God's redemptive work in Jesus. Yet if we cannot see God or our neighbour's role in God's redemptive work, then we may altogether miss out on participating in the beautiful work of God. God is transforming our neighbourhoods in the most unlikely places (like your home) and in the most creative, surprising, and humble ways (like working with you). We need eyes to see those divine invitations to join in the work of God as it unfolds in front of us.

Jesus encountered those who could not see the present and unfolding world-blessing work of God. In Matthew 15:14 Jesus had some sharp words for the religious leaders of his day when he called the Pharisees and teachers of the law "blind guides."Although they knew the law and the prophets thoroughly, these experts were unable to 'see.' Standing before them was their incarnate Lord, their long-awaited Messiah, and yet their vision was restricted by their own purposes and ambitions. In their blindness they could not see the global redemptive story playing out right before their eyes. Jewish identity was rooted in the ancient covenant God made with Abraham, a promise passed down through the generations that the whole world would be blessed through Abraham and his people (Genesis12:1-3). As Christopher J. H. Wright says, "The nations will indeed be blessed as Abraham was, but only because they will have turned to the only source of blessing, Abraham's God, and identified themselves with the story of Abraham's people."[23]

The Pharisees standing before Jesus were not identifying with Abraham's God and the grand story of God's redemptive work for the world. They simply could not imagine how Jesus would fit with their image of redemption. With their identity opaquely tarnished, and their vision of God obscured, the Pharisees fearfully resisted Jesus. Their fear and disbelief ruled their actions, and these blind leaders were left unmoved even as they faced God's own Son. Their imaginations could not see God for who he was. They were numb.

This inability to 'see' is a challenge for the church today as we seek to live out the hope of Jesus where we live. The redemptive work of God is transformative and the story profoundly central, yet week after week many churches struggle to 'see' the ways that they may be able to participate with God in God's mission. C. Baxter Kruger tells of a church where the life-giving message of the Father's love "was being obscured. And it was not because the love of God had not been proclaimed. The people knew all about the love of the Father. But still they were asleep, uninspired, fearful, timid. Something deeper was overriding the message of God's amazing love in Christ - suffocating it. ...There was another message being sounded which short circuited the liberating light."[24]

In time they found out what contributed to their inability to see. In that particular community they discovered that people had come to falsely imagine God as distant and perpetually unsatisfied with them. They had come to believe that "There is a side of God that does not like me."[25] By viewing God as a distant judge who is pained at the thought of loving them, the church was unable to step into the work of God all around them. Their imaginations were stifled by this lie and it made them timid, fearful, sleepy, and uninspired.

David Morgan describes 'seeing' as more than just laying one's eyes on something. Rather, "To see is to sense, intuit and collectively imagine what lies within or beyond an image."[26] An image alone will not create transformation, imagining, and entering into what is beyond that image will. The Pharisees knew the scriptures and could recite all the ancient texts, yet could not see themselves as part of that redemptive work of God happening before them. Similarly, the church described by Kruger was regularly presented with the hope-filled message of God, yet could not see God for who he was revealing himself to be. For the Pharisees back then and for our churches and neighborhoods today, we may require more than what words or images can sometimes offer. We need an experience of the imagination, of beauty.

It was beauty that saved me that night as I drove down the dark highway. Up until Chopin's piano music filled the car, my senses, feelings, soul, and mind were numb. I was restricted in my ability to see Jesus and respond. My identity, my purpose, my hope and my joy were all crowded out in that tight space, and there was no apparent way for me to see through it all. The experience of feeling numb or spiritually asleep is disconcerting. Feeling as though God is distant or unwilling to speak to us can make us fearful, sad, or angry. During times of pain we describe our emotional responses as 'shutting down,' 'growing cold,' or 'pushing others away.' Lastly, the loneliness can lead to forgetfulness. A sense of God's distance reinforces a false identity; we are not God's and God has no interest in us or the world we live in. We forget who we are and who God is.

There is a kind of anaesthetization that happens when blindness prevents people and communities from embracing their identity in Christ. Numbness sets in to the place where love and pain used to be, sleepiness replaces attentiveness to the work of the Spirit, fear replaces hope, and apathy becomes a substitute for life.

When we see, then;

We are reminded, then;

We step into life with confidence and trust, then;

We slow down, then;

We live open-handedly and present to others, then;

We reveal our true lives, and open our eyes some more.

Jesus calls all of us who squint in the sun-bright white of day to trust him. Don't be afraid. You can open your eyes. There's something you need to see, and it's beautiful.

Anaesthetic

"Avoid silence, avoid solitude, avoid any train of thought that leads off the beaten track.
Concentrate on money, sex, status, health and (above all) on your own grievances.
Keep the radio on. Live in a crowd. Use plenty of sedation."
-C.S. Lewis[27]

I was a teenager when my dentist told me it was time to get my wisdom teeth removed. He assured me that it was a simple surgery and some happy drugs would make sure I did not remember a thing. I was happy, but mostly because I got the afternoon off from school. When I heard that I was going to be knocked out by some drugs, I came up with a little plan, the kind that only a teenage boy might scheme. I decided I was going to beat the anaesthetic. It would be easy. With a healthy dose of willpower I could, no doubt, fight off any concoction of drugs that the dental assistant was going to use on me. The day of the surgery came and I had my whole strategy figured out. I would 'will' myself to stay awake. I would force my eyes to stay open, clench my fists, and keep talking; whatever was necessary. So after a bit of chit-chat the nurse prepped my arm for the needle. "This'll only pinch a bit." She pushed in the drug and asked me to count down from 100. With my eyes wide open and determined, and a confident smirk on my face, I began to count down.

100

99

98

Not bad so far. I figured I was doing well. This was easy.

97

It was then that I made my fatal mistake. I decided to close my eyes, just for a moment. Just a blink, really...

I woke up that afternoon in another room and realized that I had lost. The dentist was right, I did not remember a thing.

Anaesthetics are potent, as I discovered. More potent than any kind of willpower or determination on my part. There are two kinds of anaesthesia: local and general. A local anaesthetic works in a specific place to dull pain receptors. Dentists use a needle to administer an anaesthetic to a tooth before drilling or filling a cavity. The patient stays awake, but the pain is gone, or at least the pain is not felt. A general anaesthetic, however, affects the whole system by causing amnesia, suppression of responses to stimuli, unconsciousness, and immobility.[28] As I tried to fight the anaesthetic administered by the dentist, I found that I simply could not. I passed out and forgot the whole affair.

Eugene Peterson writes that, "Our senses have been dulled by sin. The world, for all its vaunted celebration of sensuality, is relentlessly anaesthetic."[29] Could Peterson be right? Could it be that the world, with its big, new homes, iPads, summer blockbuster movies, Mexican vacations, and shopping malls filled with noise and distraction is actually lacking sensuality? That for all the sensory overload, people are becoming increasingly numb to what they see and hear? A vehicle collision at an intersection is merely a novelty on the way to work, the trees and parks are just the backdrop to a busy life. The racket has turned into a hum and ringing smartphones are simply the expected soundtrack of our day. This becomes our anaesthetic as the clamour numbs our ability to be attentive. We can no longer hear the "still small voice" of the Holy Spirit above the noise.

The opposite of anaesthetic is aesthetic. The opposite of numb and sleepy is beauty and the sublime. Let that sink in for a moment. Consider that in a "relentlessly anaesthetic" world, we have the means to wake up again: it's called beauty. Art. Music. A Spouse. Tulips. Bees. Kids. Neighbours. The list is long and the more you look for beauty, the more you see. Beauty brings life. If beauty truly is the antidote to the drowsiness we feel in work, relationships, worship, and play, then we need to discover what it means to step into the beautiful; to feel, touch, taste, see, and hear every good thing that God has put before us.

My own journey towards life started in the apiary and the garden, but moved outwards towards my neighbours and community. From a small moment with an insect, to a growing vision of God at work in my neighbourhood, I have begun to see how beauty is the threshold to life. The challenge doesn't come from a lack of beauty around us, rather it is often our fear of pain that inhibits our ability to step into the beautiful world that brings us to life.

In our fear of pain, we run towards anything that will numb us down. Somewhere in the process of snipping off our nerves and burning out our feelings, we have inadvertently shut down the very things we need to find life again. To see and feel opens us to pain, it's true. But seeing and feeling are vital to experiencing beauty; and beauty is the lifeline we need. Beauty is the eye-opening jolt of hope, an appointment with God and the world that God created. The aesthetic reminds us that we are not done yet. It's the dead who no longer feel, but we are still among the living.

I hope to always turn from the anaesthetic to the aesthetic. When people learn that I'm a beekeeper, often they will lean in and ask, "Haven't you been stung?" Really what they're asking is, "Why would you subject yourself to pain like that?" It is as though a moment of pain would be enough to have me avoid the whole venture. That a bee sting would severely hamper my life and perhaps it's time to rethink my hobby. There's almost a sense of incredulity when people learn that I'm willing to subject myself to pain. Who would do such a thing? Most people, it seems to me, would be willing to forgo the potential of pain and sit in a sterile back yard, without honey bees, aromatic thorny roses, or spiny and gorgeous barberry bushes. If it could hurt, sting, or poke, avoid it. Cut off the pain, numb the nerve.

As a beekeeper, I'm willing to be stung now and then. In exchange for the rare sting, I get a front-row seat to beauty. By opting to 'feel' the bad, I get to experience so much that is good. Barbara Brown Taylor wrote that "Because it is so real, pain is an available antidote to unreality - not the medicine you would have chosen, perhaps, but an effective one all the same."[30] She rightly sees the ways in which pain snaps us to attention to the very real world around us. Manicured lawns are not the norm; nettles and wasps are. Pain is the doorway to the real life around us.

Pain may be an antidote to unreality, but experiencing beauty counters the anaesthetic we use to numb the pain. I do not dwell on the stinging honey bee, even though it catches my attention once in awhile. My eyes are set, rather, on the beautiful world they indwell and create all around me. It is beauty that makes everything come alive.

The Beautiful Ones

"High and dry, out of the rain; it's so easy to hurt others when you can't feel pain."
- *Rich Girl* by Hall and Oates

Over and over again the Bible nudges us towards the fact that people are deeply and inherently valuable in the eyes of God. Mysteriously, we are made in God's image, and somehow we are so dear to our Creator that God has made a way for us to be with God now and forever. Yet you would not get that message by watching the news or overhearing neighbours talk about each other. In our anaesthetically numb culture, the world is increasingly uninspired by the miracle of God's image reflected in each person. Instead of seeing the beauty in people, individuals are viewed through the de-humanizing lenses of social status, efficiency, and productivity. Sterile job titles, political positions, age, gender, and religious affiliations all serve to help an anaesthetized culture conveniently put people in their appropriate boxes and categories so that we can move on to whatever business is at hand. This business turns to busy-ness and becomes the anaesthetic for a world that has forgotten its identity. Forgetfulness has made us numb and busyness has made us forget. It is a closed cycle. Like a needle in the arm and a countdown from 100, there is little we can do to stand against the powerful effects of the anaesthetics that surround us.

Anaesthetics are well-known to our culture. Daryl Hall and John Oates, those popular philosophers of 1980s soft rock, wrote a song called *Rich Girl*. The song takes a swipe at a rich girl who has everything. They sing, "High and dry, out of the rain; it's so easy to hurt others when you can't feel pain." She has everything she wants, so much so that she's become numb to the emotions of others. The song continues, "You can get along if you try to be strong but you'll never be strong 'cause you're a rich girl." This complete abundance of material wealth has made the 'rich girl' weak. Hall and Oates see the cultural malady for what it is. This 'rich girl' cannot feel pain nor can she ever be strong. She is anaesthetized now so move along, there's nothing surprising here.[31]

The list of anaesthetics we face everyday is long. Almost anything around us can be used to numb our pain or put us to sleep. Daily we are offered technologies, activities, or products to distract us when something in life is painful. We each have ways to numb life's disappointments, frustrations, or sadness. Sometimes we just need a big pizza and a Netflix marathon to unwind, and often that's OK. Our anaesthetics, however, can numb us in ways we didn't expect. What began as a stress-buster can, over time, turn into something more. A few grade five students at our local elementary school recently made a presentation to their fellow students about the pitfalls of videogame addictions. These students found that in some cases they're used in unhealthy ways. They can be a numbing anaesthetic that many kids turn to that could interfere with relationships and harm their physical and emotional health.

Anaesthetics could go even deeper. Over years a married couple may choose to speak less and less to each other. In a strained work environment a coworker may shut down. A teenager may close off the world. Your neighbour may keep to himself. This kind of separation and division is yet another anaesthetic. In lives hurt by bad experiences, sometimes the easiest solution is to shut out the other person, avoid the conversation, and close shop. When we start to see the world through this lens it becomes apparent that we are numb and sleepy - and many would prefer to keep it that way.

If we are bombarded by anaesthetics, and if many of us believe we have found our eternal happy-place parked in front of the distraction of our choosing, how could we possibly find life again? How do we 'wake up'? We wake up not by our own willpower, not by a strategy, not from a skillset. We wake up by exposure to beauty.

Fyodor Dostoevsky once wrote in his novel *The Idiot* that "beauty will save the world."[32] It was a line spoken by one of my favourite characters, Prince Myshkin, who was a virtual nobody and affectionately called an 'idiot'. Myshkin was surrounded by people who flaunted their wealth and stature; they relied on the vain pursuits of their high Russian society to construct their own shallow identities. Myshkin stood out from the crowd because he was strangely kind, wise, attentive, present, and non-threatening. Maybe he was a simpleton, but it didn't matter. He was no threat to the powerful and so moved freely among those clamouring towards the next fix. He was a boy who could 'see' among a society of people who were asleep. He could 'feel' when others were numb.

This enigmatic phrase, "beauty will save the world," stands out as a summary of what Dostoevsky saw as a healing salve for a world made callous to their God-created humanity. In the midst of the chaos, shame, self-satisfaction, and sorrow stood one person who saw the only thing that could bring life – and that was beauty. It should come as no surprise that Myshkin is a Christ-figure in Dostoyevsky's book, living a redemptive and beautiful life. For years after first reading *The Idiot* I felt a strange love and admiration for Myshkin and still do today. A part of me wants to be just like him.

There is a reason why Myshkin was called 'the idiot.' Those who are snapped awake by something truly beautiful are sometimes viewed as the odd person out. Hans Von Balthasar said that "both the person who is transported by natural beauty and the one snatched up by the beauty of Christ must appear to the world to be fools ..."[33] Those who are awakened by beauty begin to see through new lenses. They are discovering that beauty awakens them to God's creative and dynamic handiwork all around them.

You can spot those people in the neighbourhood who have become like Myshkin, those alert and attentive people that this book is all about. They may look like fools when they jump up and down with joy over hearing the good news about their neighbour's toddler down the street having just taken her first steps. They may be viewed as overly sentimental when they bake cookies for the family that lost their cat. Those who find life in God's beautiful work in their midst, on their street, and in their neighbourhood are those who join in the rhythm of God's beautiful work. They are the crazy ones. They step into beauty and find it. They know in their very core, and feel it in the world around them, that God is up to something profound. They want to be a part of it. Awake to it, every moment of every day.

Here is a strange way of putting it: we need a sensuous cognition of God in our neighbourhood. In other words, we need all of our senses to be alive in order to truly embrace what God is doing around us. It is in the engaging of our eyes, ears, nose, taste buds, and hands that we find beauty in our lives. Beauty can take many forms; maybe it's a walk through the neighbourhood, a backyard barbeque with friends, or a living room dance party with our kids. Maybe we take a picnic down to the overgrown community park, stay up late and listen to the distant coyotes, or plan a special date with our spouse. Finding and enjoying the beauty around us, in our family, and in our neighbourhood, may be the most awakening and life-giving posture we can take. This is the posture of those who know that the God of beauty is bringing life right where they are.

Yet beauty may be more than a moment in the park or a lovely song on the radio. In the story of Jesus we meet Thomas, a follower of Jesus who will go down in history as the guy who had a hard time believing the story that his friends were telling him. I feel for Thomas. When Jesus rose from the dead, the Bible says that Thomas didn't believe that Jesus was alive. His nickname became Doubting Thomas. He needed to touch Jesus for himself before he could accept the truth. When he finally touched Jesus for himself, his eyes were opened, his faith restored, his life renewed. Malcolm Guite wrote a poem about Thomas the Doubter:

"We cannot love some disembodied wraith,
But flesh and blood must be our King of Kings.
Your teaching is to touch, embrace, anoint,
Feel after him and find him in the flesh."[34]

Thomas could not 'see' Jesus until he touched him and embraced him for himself. It is a similar position for most people. They can be told a thousand times that God loves them and that God is making all things new and that the Kingdom of God is near. Yet until they experience God's love in tangible, hands-on, embraceable ways, they will continue to doubt. Beauty may need to come in the form of a person, in the shape of a warm-bodied, running-shoe-wearing, lame-joke-telling, spearmint-gum-chewing human being. The beauty your neighbourhood needs may be you.

This may not look like the picture of beauty we expect. You may not be the picture of beauty that you expect. Here's the surprise: Jesus indwells his people and creates beauty and life in our midst. In every diet-coke-drinking, anxiety-wrestling person who trusts Jesus, God's Spirit is present. Jesus is making himself known in you and through you. As you live into who Jesus says you are (even on your worst day) and join with God in the beauty God is creating, you demonstrate the beauty and goodness of God in the place where you live. You may come to know that it is not enough to just stand off and admire what God is doing. You, like Jesus, become part of a whole body of people, fools who jump up and down when they see beauty. You come to discover that you want more, you want in on the beautiful action. You want to become part of those who God has called to life, awakened to beauty.

Making the Invisible Visible: Beauty

At the core of this book is a desire to change the way we see our neighbours. Inherent in our neighbours is a beauty that many do not see. We truly need to be the vital and attentive people who are reshaping our own ability to see what few others do. How do we make the invisible beauty in our neighbourhoods visible to all?

Beauty is the means by which we wake up. Here are three practices that alert us to the invisible beauty all around us.

1. Beautiful prayer: Henri Nouwen in his little book, *Behold the Beauty of the Lord*, writes about a period in his life when prayer was nearly impossible. The fatigue he felt made him feel despair and fear. It was time spent sitting in front of the icon of the Holy Trinity by Andrew Rublev that his viewing slowly turned to praying. Something about the beauty of what he saw gave him words. He said, "This silent prayer slowly made my inner restlessness melt away and lifted me up into the circle of love."35

What is it about Chopin on the radio, or a 15th century painting, that can open up a person to pray again? Why do we need music, drama, visual art, poetry, and story to help us when God is, after all, only a prayer away? What is it about the beautiful hands-on love of a friend or good gut-laughter around a table that makes God and God's world come alive to us again? Some of our most profound moments with God have happened when something beautiful brought our imaginations to life. Think of a time when something beautiful brought you life. How could you incorporate beauty into a time of prayer?

2.   Listen for beauty: Eugene Peterson wrote that, "Artists make us insiders to the complexity and beauty of what we deal with every day but so often miss. They bring to our attention what is right before our eyes, within reach of our touch, help us hear sounds and combinations of sounds that our noise-deafened ears have never heard."[36] Think of the ways that you have been 'noise-deafened' by the world you live in. Even now, what sounds are filling your life and distracting you? Go for a walk through your neighbourhood. Listen for the sounds that you would normally never consider. Read John 5:19, 30 where Jesus 'sees' and 'hears' what the Father is doing. As you are attentive to these sounds? What is the Father showing and telling you about what he is doing in the neighbourhood he loves?

3.   Beautiful meal: Caring for others and offering hospitality are indicative of the life of God's people. By inviting others around our table and enjoying time around the tables of those in our neighbourhood, we are engaging in beauty. What would it mean for you to create beauty with your barbeque or crockpot this week? How would inviting neighbours to eat with you bring life to your home? I recommend hosting a soup night for the people on your street. The book *Soup Night* by Maggie Stuckey is a great resource to get you started.[37]

Awe

Awe

"How blue is the sea, how blue is the sky,
how blue and tiny and redeemable everything is, even you,
even your eyes, even your imagination."
-Mary Oliver[38]

The journey towards seeing God at work in our neighbourhood begins when we posture ourselves to participate in what God is doing around us. For many, our imaginations are not primed to see our neighbours as we pass by on our way to work. All too often the people around us are incidental to our hurried lives and seldom factor in to the daily decisions we make. Becoming keystone people, people of grace, and participants with Jesus in God's unfolding Kingdom may first require us to confess that we are numb and forgetful. In our tiredness we do not easily see the goodness that is growing around us. Yet as beauty takes hold of our hearts and imaginations, we begin to wake up to a whole new world. We become discoverers of a new way of living with Jesus, allowing him to shape our lives, loving our neighbours as he does.

The first posture is an extension of awakening beauty. When we experience beauty we need to respond by turning our attention towards this good thing we see before us. This new responsive turning is the posture of 'awe.' Awe is that heart-quickening, skin-tingling sense of appreciation for something so beautiful that it takes our breath away. It might be small and sublime or truly life-changing and splendidly glorious. I stood in awe under the stars at a Bible camp as a boy, for the first time truly believing that Jesus loved me. It was in a striking moment when I first realized just how profoundly gracious God was to bring my wife Kelly to me in a moment when I felt God had forgotten my name. I cried when I held my baby girl for the first time; with tears running down my cheeks I wondered if perhaps there could be no better moment. Once alert to beauty, awe is the full appreciation and wonder that follows.

Awe is an essential posture. Without it we could be surrounded by beauty but never truly be moved in any life-shaping way. We could be firsthand witnesses to a miraculous moment but never appreciate a second of it. Awe requires that we enter into the world around us, aware of beauty, with imaginations primed and expectant for God to show up.

Awe was that feeling I had when I saw the inside of a beehive, close up, for the first time. Yet, as a beekeeper, awe has become more global than that. It is awesome to consider that these pollinators are connected to the world of plants, food, birds, farmers, land, and the intricate and good world God created. In a similar way, I am also starting to see my neighbourhood as more than a row of houses full of nameless families. Rather, they are part of a beautiful, living, and beloved creation that God made and sustains with love and deep affection. But it was when I sat with these bees and allowed this sense of awe to alight upon my imagination that I began to truly lean into this quickening sense that something good and wonderful was happening all around me. God was here, and it was awesome.

Yet many of us have not felt a sense of awe for a very long time. Even in places where awe should be commonplace, it is missing. Nowhere is our deficient sense of awe more evident than in an airport. It is interesting to observe the way people move through airports and board their planes. Flying in a plane should be mind-bogglingly awesome, but often it doesn't feel like it. Most frequent travellers will know the routine quite well. Before ever getting on an airplane, travellers are herded through gates, checkpoints, and security stations. The dehumanizing process takes most of the joy out of traveling even before the journey begins. Like cattle, 'guests' are given a number, encouraged along at an efficient pace, and then set up in rows to wait for the 'deplaning' travellers.

The only people having a good time are the kids, who in their enthusiasm are plastered against the window at the gate, wide-eyed at the majestic airplane parked just outside. They have the capacity to dream about life in the sky. They still have that sense of anticipation that they are about to experience some form of magic, a thrill of wonder (or at least the kids who are not already glued to their iPads). Everyone else is checking emails or looking for a place to charge their phones.

Then, after a tedious wait, the call is made and groups of travellers board the airplane. As each person settles into their seat, one look around and the case is made - any kind of awe has been completely stripped from the imagination of most passengers. They flip through magazines, surf the internet, or close their window shade in preparation for what still must be the most amazing experience created by modern humanity: air travel.

Flying at 40,000 feet at about 500 miles per hour, airplanes are aluminum tubes jetting through sub-zero, low-oxygen conditions, in almost complete safety. Using complex, globally-connected computers, advancements in material science, and with the favourable conditions that come from modern economics, geopolitical stability, and an educated, literate work force, we are able to fly thousands of people across the world every day. In all of human history, billions of people have not experienced speed or flight, and yet in mere decades, air travel has become so ubiquitous that we don't even pay attention to it, let alone marvel at it. The sheer number of factors that have come together to allow people to watch a movie way up in the sky is almost incalculable, and yet we barely notice or care. No awe here, we guess.

And yet it is there. We see it in the eyes of children. They dream about their flight before and after. The experience of flight is awesome; children know this full well. The challenge is not in creating a more awe-inspiring experience, rather that air travellers ought to consider pausing to appreciate what they have just encountered. They need to posture themselves, like kids, in a way that momentarily embraces the magic of the moment.

A few years ago I took a group of people to visit Israel. We were going to travel around, learn, and take in all the sights and sounds - to experience life as Jesus might have. Preparing people to travel overseas can be a lot of work as group members ask questions about attire, spending money, and sleeping arrangements. When our itinerary showed that we might have a longer layover in Germany, the group groaned. "Couldn't we get a more direct flight?" someone asked. So I did the one thing that always changes the tone of the conversation. I decided to pull out some accounts of pilgrimages from the Middle Ages. I told stories of faithful Christians who would sell their entire family estate to afford the three-month journey by boat to Palestine. Many Christians would pull into the harbour at Joppa then spend days securing a donkey ride to Jerusalem. Once in Jerusalem, the political climate was so risky that all the pilgrims were often locked into the Church of the Holy Sepulchre overnight to sleep on floors. Historians recount how the church was a haven for fleas and disease. After a few days of prayer, pilgrims would make their way back to the harbour. Along the way many would be robbed. One recounted how they were stabbed, and still others found themselves too weak to manage. By the time they would get on a boat for the return journey, they were penniless with nothing but mouldy bread and fleas for company.

Yet these early pilgrims understood the importance of awe. They gave all of their earthly treasures for a taste of it.

A pilgrimage to Jerusalem or modern air travel might not inspire much awe in you. But it begins to make you wonder, what does inspire us?

Hunting for Awe

Where do we find awe? David Yaden and Johannes Eichstaedt at the University of Pennsylvania have been studying the surprising, and often overwhelming, sense of awe experienced by astronauts as they look down on the planet from the International Space Station. They analyzed statements from the scientists and came to the conclusion that awe was the most apt word to describe their feelings. They found that "themes emerged from the quotes, ideas like unity, vastness, connectedness, perception — in general, this sense of an overwhelming, life-changing moment." These university researchers did not expect to find so much awe expressed in this highly scientific and secular environment. They wrote that "we don't [often] think of these very strict scientists reporting these blissful moments." Yet there it was: awe.

In the scientific, secular, and regimented environment of the International Space Station, even the most analytical mind is overcome by awe. Awe is not merely the realm of children or spiritually artsy people, it is the capacity that everyone has to stand alert and attentive to majestic beauty. These researchers conclude that a sense of awe may be transformative. These experiences, they say, "help people in some ways be more adaptive, feel more connected, reframe troubles."[39] As Chinese astronaut Yang Liu said after viewing earth from above, "I had another feeling, that the Earth is like a vibrant, living thing. ... I said to myself: this is the place we live, it's really magical."[40] Awe is a universal response to what we see that has the capability to deeply shape our imaginations, and in turn, shape the way we live.

Frederick Buechner told a story about Paul Tillich, a theologian, who would stand in awe of the ocean. Buechner wrote that,

"he would pile up a mound of sand and sit on it gazing out at the ocean with tears running down his cheeks. One wonders what there was about it that moved him so. The beauty and power of it? The inexpressible mystery of it? The futility of all those waves endlessly flowing in and ebbing out again? Who knows? Maybe it was when he looked at the ocean that he caught a glimpse of the One he was praying to. Maybe what made him weep was how vast and overwhelming it was and yet at the same time as near as the breath of it in his nostrils, as salty as his own tears."[41]

Standing before a vast ocean inspires awe, and in some moments we, too, may stand breathless in wonder at the God who made such a majestic expanse.

When I ask my classes to describe an awe moment, I will most often get a comment about mountains or nature. Nature frequently inspires awe. After weeks, months, or years in a concrete jungle, there is no doubt that a hike in the Rocky Mountains does produce a relieving sense of awe in me. The crisp air, beautiful scenery, and picturesque vistas are enough to refresh me like few other experiences. I'm not alone. Philosophers such as Joseph Addison and John Dennis who, in the 18th century traveled through the Alps, stood with a particular kind of awe. They believed that the Alps were more than beautiful, they were sublime. The mountains had a quality that was immeasurably better than what we might call beauty. They had a splendour that was simply beyond imitation and beyond words. For them, no manmade art could ever be called sublime. It was a word that could only be reserved for the very highest forms of natural beauty, for mountains and other marvels of creation.

This sense of awe appears over and over again in Scripture. Throughout the Psalms we see the way in which the heavens were a deep source of wonder. Psalm 19: 4-6 says, "God has made a home in the heavens for the sun. It bursts forth like a radiant bridegroom after his wedding. It rejoices like a great athlete eager to run the race. The sun rises at one end of the heavens and follows its course to the other end." Who has not surrendered their gaze and awe to the vast field of stars or the dancing northern lights? There is something disarmingly beautiful about creation.

Advances in technology have further expanded our ability to stand in awe of the cosmos. The Hubble Space Telescope has, for the past 20 years, returned images of space that have been stunning. From expanding space clouds made up of millions of stars, to galaxy clusters that defy the imagination's ability to make sense of their sheer scope and scale. With new telescopes set to come online in the near future, space science will continue to inspire awe.

In my own back yard I have a surprising source of continual awe. Tens of thousands of honey bees zip in and out of my hive, intent on their duties and tasks. Some researchers now believe that honey bees, which have seed-sized brains, are able to compute in an instant what our fastest computers might compute over several days.[42] They have a capacity for global positioning, communication, cooperation, defence, sacrifice, and efficiency that rival the most advanced species. There are days when I forget all of this and lose my own awe for bees. Then my daughter wiggles her way onto our garden bench and discovers the beauty of bees. She sits there enraptured in sheer astonishment over these bugs shooting past her, through the flowers, and up and over the fence into the neighbourhood. She sits there in awe.

Recently I took my daughter to a bird sanctuary. It was late in the season and most birds had moved on to warmer climates. But we were told that if we looked closely, we would see more than ponds and pathways. So we looked. On my way through the bird sanctuary I came across a little sign. It read,

> "It's not what you look at that matters, it's what you see."
> -Henry David Thoreau

Very few people were at the bird sanctuary, but we did come across a few photographers with three-foot-long lenses looking up in the leafless trees. "There's usually some owls around here," one of them told me. A few kids in a school group shuffled by, vaguely flipping through their workbooks and snickering about some inside jokes. My little girl, a toddler, found a spot by a footbridge where she could throw leaves into the pond and watch them float along. I was looking for evidence of beavers among the many beaver trails and fallen trees. We were looking at the same space, but seeing very different things. The little sign was right, we are all looking at the same space, but are we seeing what really matters?

In a world that is home to mountains and honey bees, set with a backdrop of near infinite stars and galaxies, we may find ourselves at home with some small, intermittent sense of awe. But what we look at may not be what we need to see. Perhaps the sublime is not only found in the mountains or even in paintings of the mountains. Perhaps the most beautiful thing we can see is much more closer to home. What if our hunt for true awe brings us to those living right next door?

People are sublime.

For all the beauty of mountains and space, I am discovering that people are the most sublime. Yes, strangely I've come to believe that boring, frustrating, and annoying humans are perhaps the pinnacle of all that is wonderful and good in the world. This may be surprising to some; people seem to be so common. An hour stuck in traffic can almost make us feel like other humans are simply part of the mundane fabric of the world around us, nowhere close to the breathtaking experience we think would be associated with awe. Give us mountains and beauty, not people. Stick with stars, birds, and bees. That's the good stuff. Yet even from space, astronauts stare in awe at both the beauty and the fragility of the people too small to see. These mundane, boring, insignificant people may in fact ignite the highest sense of awe a person might experience.

I've often felt that mountains are not the pinnacle of beauty in the world, that they are not the most meaningful source of spiritual awe and satisfaction. Neither are bees, or birds, or stars. I leave the mountains with renewed life, but I return to my neighbourhood and city to encounter the most stunning source of beauty in its most sublime form: people. Eugene Peterson, a spiritual theologian who loves nature and beauty wrote that "Even a bare-bones human existence contains enough glory to stagger any one of us into bewildered awe."[43] Just by their very being, people proclaim something astonishing about the world we live in.

Not convinced? Read on.

Ali Binazir, an author and mathematician, was so astonished by how rare and beautiful people are that he wrote, in a whimsical article on the Harvard Law blog, about the chances of you and me coming into existence. He worked out the numbers and found that the mathematical likelihood of any person being born is about 1 in $10^{2,685,000}$. According to Binazir, the chances of your mom and dad meeting were about 1 in 20,000, then figure in the chances of just the right combination of sperm and egg connecting on just the right day, and our numbers jump to about 1 in 400 quadrillion. Considering that this had to happen just right across generations, while avoiding disease, war, and famine, and you'll see the sheer unlikeliness that you should even exist. It is simply staggering. Your chances of being here are about one in $10^{2,685,000}$.

To get our head around that number, let's consider that there are about this many atoms that make up planet earth: 133,000,000,000,000,000,000,000,000,000,000,000,000,000,000,000,00 0. That's 133 with 48 zeros after it. But our number is so much bigger. Our number has millions of zeros after it. Enough zeros that you would need a bookshelf to contain all the zeros if they were written out on paper. Ali Binazir says, "So, what's the probability of your existing? It's the probability of 2 million people getting together – about the population of San Diego – each to play a game of dice with trillion-sided dice. They each roll the dice, and they all come up with the exact same number – say, 550,343,279,001."[44]

It is astonishing to me to think that the person reading this now (you!) are a rare, unique, utterly beautiful, mind-bendingly sublime person. You are handmade by God under conditions beyond our understanding. No mountain or telescope can compare to the sense of 'awe' that we should have when we think about the chances of our coming into existence. Without having accomplished so much as a breath, even babies command our attention, causing us to marvel in awe at God's amazing creation.

Time and time again people, like me, have been surprised to discover that the most beautiful thing they could discover is another person. Vincent Van Gogh who famously painted stars and beauty in nature said that "I feel that there is nothing more truly artistic than to love people." [45] His love of nature brought him to a place where he could stand in awe of the people around him.

Humans, for all of their flaws and brokenness, still carry within them this beautiful and strange truth: they are made in the image of God. We reflect, in some mysterious way, qualities and characteristics of God. Generosity is a reflection of God's character, and our neighbour embodies that every time they let you borrow their extra long ladder. There's a very kind young boy who lives down our street. Every time I see the way he treats small kids and toddlers, I'm reminded that he's reflecting God's image every time he passes a soccer ball to one of the other kids. Nothing else in all of creation is described in the Bible in quite the way that people are. People best reflect the character and image of God, and some of those reflections are found right next door.

What does it mean to see others as made in the image of God? Lewis B. Smedes said,
"We must see every person as someone who lives each moment in relationship with God. We need to see the religious connection if we want to recognize the essence of human sacredness. The concrete person, beautiful or ugly, productive or idle, smart or stupid, is the one God made, whom God loves, whose life is in God's hands, and for whom his Son died on the cross. This is the person who walks humbly on the earth as the image and likeness of the Creator who made him." [46]

Whether it is a mountain, space, or the amazing uniqueness of people, we do not lack the inspiration for awe. All around us is a world, created by God, that stands on interactive display, declaring beauty, and showcasing the sublime. What is lacking is our ability to see and stand in awe of what is unfolding and blooming before us.

When we step out onto our front porch we often only see a row of houses, a few cars, and maybe that stray cat. We are hardly inspired to see our neighbours as anything other than mere people who live down our street. But when we begin to cultivate a sense of awe for the world around us, the people on our block begin to take on a new vibrancy. Jesus' command to love our neighbour sounds less like a dull duty and more like an invitation into relationship with God's most astonishing, sublime creation. Even wounded, used, and broken versions of God's creation should draw out wordless awe from each of us. That kid who ran across your lawn is a one-of-a-kind, deeply loved, and adored person who was created in the image of God. Be in awe of those around you and you'll learn about the character and nature of God at work in you.

Making the Invisible Visible: Awe

When we begin to see the world outside our front door with new awe-shaped lenses, loving our neighbours is not a chore but a delight. Putting ourselves out there to engage and love our neighbourhoods is not a numbing task but an extension of this deep sense of the beauty that is just below the surface, if only we could see it. These experimental postures and practices are intended to help you see your neighbours with awe and hopefully come to experience the wonder of the world around you in new and life-giving ways.

1. Better than royalty: Chances are you live better than most kings and queens of centuries past. The home you live in has more luxuries and amenities than nearly any palace in ancient times. Your refrigerator and pantry very likely have more variety of foods of a much better quality than anything the kings of France had ever enjoyed. The fact that your life expectancy is likely somewhere above 70 makes your health better than anything the rulers of ancient Egypt ever looked forward to. By recognizing that our lives rival the best lives of the most privileged people in the history of humanity should give us a moment of pause. We have been given the lives of kings and queens, and yet we seldom stand in awe of our privilege. Take time today to count the ways that you live a life of luxury and ease. Recognize that this is a gift. What will you do with it?

2. Crying babies: Each newborn baby is a fresh reflection of God. The Bible says that we are made in the Image of God. Even at our most raw

and incapable (crying babies fit the bill for me!), we declare the goodness of God. This week, identify the least impressive and the least able person in your world. Spend some time with them and turn your attention to the ways that they are made in the Image of God. With these new lenses, begin to look for the ways that God's character is found in others, in your neighbours, and in your own life. When we practice looking for it, we begin to re-form awe in our imaginations.

3. Start small: Become a child again. Sometimes it helps to take kids along for this lesson. Go on a scavenger hunt at a local park or forest. Take time to re-engage with the beauty around you in the small things. Celebrate over the discovery of a bug, or the world of life under a rock. I love heading out with my nieces to hunt for a 'Geocache' (geocaching.com). The goal of this exercise is to remind your imagination to continually connect with little wonders. By doing so, God may begin to reveal the larger wonders of those whom God loves next door.

4. Spotting the miraculous: As a boy I used to think that trees were probably a miracle that humans simply got too used to. Imagine if in some other world, where trees did not exist, one finally grew from the ground. It would be a miracle of the highest order. How many miracles surround you each day that you've simply gotten used to? How many wonders dot your path to work and play? When we spot the small miracles, they grow in size and our imaginations are reshaped to accommodate them in all of their glory. Start first by spotting the miracle of the bird or the tree, then move on to people. You may see that next door lives a miracle of the highest order; and if so, what does that change in you?

5. Surprise: Surprise Industries (surpriseindustries.com), is a movement and a book aimed at recapturing the joy of being surprised. Its creators believe that we can embrace unpredictable moments and engineer the unexpected. Consider the ways that you may have lost the feeling of surprise and consider how rediscovering surprise in your city may lead you to see the ways that God is at work all around you.

Security

Security

When I first became a beekeeper, my sense of security was set at level 11. I did not want to get stung and I was convinced that all bees were likely out to get me. So I bought a full, head-to-toe beekeepers suit, the mesh hood, the gloves, the whole package. In fact, I bought two suits, just in case. I wore work boots and fired up my smoker. I didn't want a single bee getting in, so I wrapped duct tape around my ankles. I used every trick I could find to ensure that these stinging bugs would not hurt me.

Today I know much more about honey bees. I know when they may feel threatened and when they are docile. I know their sounds and behaviours, and the more I know about them, the more I've adjusted my approach to safety. Even my daughter has taken cues from me and knows when it's perfectly fine to go up to a beehive and when to stay a few feet away. I am aware of the dangers, and it is important not to be flippant around honey bees. However my familiarity and love for these garden pollinators has drastically changed my activities in the apiary. I'm careful but relaxed, open, and able to enjoy this beautiful gift.

Our sense of security shapes our posture towards others and our neighbourhoods. How we understand our security and our relationships with our neighbours will lead us either closer to, or away from, the people who live around us. The beliefs we form about our security are shaped within us for our protection. That's why we're taught at a young age to avoid strangers and to lock our doors. However some security postures we take may not lead us towards the kind of security we may need if we're to live openly and lovingly towards our neighbours. Our desire for heightened security may have helped us avoid getting in a car with a stranger when we were kids, but the way our imaginations were shaped when we were young may create a kind of self-preservation that today actually turns us away from others. We might be turning away the very people God is inviting into our lives.

In our own neighbourhoods we each have a posture of security towards our neighbours. Whether instilled in us while we are young or learned after a couple of bad experiences, we develop our own security system. We lock our doors and cars, set alarms, build fences, look out through our blinds at some movement down the street, and carefully engage in small talk with those who walk by. In Canada, at least, many have learned how to be polite without letting their guard down. We'll stand around the mailbox, but we might not sit around the kitchen table. We're cautious, and this maintains our sense of security. Whenever I teach about security and the need to revisit the way we think about our own security in our neighbourhoods, I can see how it makes some people uncomfortable. It is not easy to rethink our sense of security. As watch-from-the-window neighbours, we will often ensure that our security posture is kept in place, solid, and safe.

It was through years of experience in the apiary that I changed my posture towards bees. Over time, familiarity with and love for the bees slowly changed the way I responded to them. I no longer needed the big bee suit or the gloves, I could let my guard down. I could enjoy my bees a little more closely. Soon I discovered that I could feel the same with those on my street. Familiarity and love changed the way I understood my own sense of security practices in my neighbourhood. In both beekeeping and neighbouring, familiarity and love are foundational. Both find their roots, and their growth, in an environment of trust. When trust is found and fostered, amazing things begin to happen.

One inspiring experiment in trust comes from one of the most corrupt nations in the world. Indonesia was ranked 114/177 on the corruption scale in 2013[47], and over 90 per cent of Indonesians said that corruption was widespread throughout their government.[48] When compared to my country, Canada, which is ninth on the scale and one of the least corrupt in the world, it's hard to imagine a place where you always need to be on your guard from con artists, criminals, police, and government officials. Beyond corruption there is also the threat of extremism; the abduction of foreigners and terrorism are an ongoing threat in Indonesia. It is not a place known for security and safety.

The common solutions for these kinds of security problems and dishonest gain would typically include more stricter law enforcement and harsher penalties. But in 2009 Indonesian anti-corruption officials and local entrepreneurs worked together to come up with a new solution to the rampant problems facing their society. They opened up "Honesty Cafes." These are small open-air shops with shelves full of drinks and snacks but no cashier. Patrons are encouraged to pay the right amount by putting their coins in a dish and take only the food they paid for - all in good faith. In a society threatened by corruption, theft, and dishonesty, you may expect this to be a doomed business plan, but it was not. One student who regularly uses the cafe said, "This motivates us to be honest, especially since there is a lot of cheating in class, at least we're learning to be honest with money. I think it's also important for society because corruption is a big problem in Indonesia." Although about five per cent of the shops incurred a loss, the vast majority were successful. Those running the program believe that these countercultural honesty cafes are actually changing behaviours in the larger society. The shops are set up in schools and government buildings, and proponents believe that values of honesty are actually working their way into the classroom and offices as a result of small acts of trust.[49] Could trust really be the solution to a nation-wide culture of insecurity?

In Canada we may not have widespread corruption or live in fear of being abducted, but we are a guarded, careful, and hyper-secure nation in other, perhaps more subtle, ways. We carry mobile phones to ensure our constant communication with those around us. We build retirement savings to shore up financial security. We set aside dog parks to keep pets in a designated place, and fences to keep neighbours and their prying eyes out of our business. We lock doors, close garages, fill shopping carts, buy new cars, go to church, and take vacations, all to ensure our property, travel, kitchen table, faith, and leisure are securely under our capable control. And at the end of the day when our neighbourhood is locked down and each resident is securely in their own home, we stand back and admire our well-ordered community. But is this what makes a neighbourhood? Are we setting up an environment where we can love our neighbours and live into the Kingdom of God together? Or are we guided more by our insecurities than our call to join in the beautiful mission of God? Do we step into the world as Jesus did, or step out of it?

Paul Born, a community organizer, told me a story about the opportunities he has to consult with police organizations around the world. He often asks them, "What makes a community safe?" He says that the police groups always reply, "It depends." The single factor, according to police around the world, that keeps a community safe depends on this: how much neighbours care for one another. And neighbours who care for each other are also those who care about their city, their kids, whether their neighbour's garage door is open when it normally wouldn't be, and are alert to suspicious activity on their street. Paul Born said that thieves really do not like spending time in neighbourhoods where people care for each other. High levels of personal neighbourhood engagement translates into lower levels of crime.

John McKnight and Peter Block, in writing about what makes a neighbourhood safe, say that, "No number of gates or professional security people on patrol can make us safe. They can increase arrests, but basically safety is in the hands of citizens. Citizens outside the house, interacting with others, being familiar with the comings and goings of the neighbors."[50] We live with a false sense of security when we lock our doors, charge our cell phones, build a fence, or change the password. Like the Indonesian communities dealing with corruption and crime, the solution to our need for safety and security comes not from better alarm systems but from an engagement and attentiveness to the world around us. In a word, true security comes from building trust. When we begin to discover that we need to become agents of trust in our neighbourhoods, we set aside the itch to serve ourselves first, and instead begin to live into the places where God is at work and where life is taking root in our communities.

In-secure Jesus

"Go and do the same."
- Jesus

Jesus often addressed the question of security through the telling of stories. In Luke 10 we read about the disciples going out to face some of their own moments of insecurity. They are receiving hospitality, staying with strangers, and sharing the message of the Kingdom of God. Then an expert of the law asks Jesus, 'Who is my neighbour?" and Jesus tells a story. He tells of a group of people who passed a man beaten and penniless on the side of the road. It's the story of the Good Samaritan. A priest and a Levite both passed the man on the other side of the road. We are not told their motivations for avoiding the dying man, but we can assume that stopping to help this filthy nobody was not a very safe thing to do. It was out of a desire for security, safeguarding their time, resources, emotions, even religious status, that they crossed to the other side. But the Samaritan was not concerned about his security, he touched the dirty man and used his own time and money to care for him.

By avoiding the man on the road and saving their own integrity, we might say that the priest and Levite remained safe and secure. The fact that the Samaritan opened himself to risk, we might say that he was not secure. But the opposite is true. It is out of their insecurity and fears that the priest and Levite were unwilling to help. It was out of scarcity of resources that they avoided this interaction. The Samaritan was actually the one who exhibited a sense of security. He did not view his resources as scarce or his own personal wellbeing as a something worth safeguarding at the expense of the dying man.

Jesus, in telling the story, says that each passerby 'saw' the man dying. The priest "saw the man lying there" (Luke 10:31), the second man "looked at him" (Luke 10:32), and the Samaritan "saw the man" (Luke 10:33). Each observed the situation. They took in the circumstances. So often Jesus is reminding his listeners that they may see with their eyes but still be blind to what God is doing. In Matthew 13:13 Jesus says, "That is why I use these parables, for they look, but they don't really see. They hear, but they don't really listen or understand." Although each of the characters in Jesus' story saw the same dying man, they each responded differently. The priest and the Levite both avoided the situation. For many political and religious reasons, it was a dangerous move to care for the man. Kenneth Bailey says that "the decision was freighted with danger." To serve in the temple after being defiled by a dying man would make the priest unfit to serve and he could face court charges or even death. So there is no doubt that the priest and the Levite were making the safe move in steering clear. The Samaritan saw the same situation and instead "felt compassion for him" (v.33). After taking care of the man's wounds, he loaded him on his donkey, and took him to an inn. This also has worrisome implications. Bailey puts it this way, "A Samaritan would not be safe in a Jewish town with a wounded Jew over the back of his riding animal. Community vengeance may be enacted against the Samaritan..."[51] So all three travellers faced significant risks to their security by caring for the dying man. Yet one person, the Samaritan, saw the situation differently and put his own security in its right perspective.

Jesus reinforces the point that it was the Samaritan who was the good neighbour, that he was the one who took the appropriate risk, and that we should do likewise. The Samaritan's clear understanding of security allowed him to see what was happening, step into the moment and then respond. Jesus said that this is what makes him a good neighbour. Take a look at this comparison. The priest and the Levite demonstrated all the characteristics of safe and secure travellers, and yet the Samaritan was actually the one who lived with a deep sense of security.

Priest and Levite	Samaritan
Gave no time	Gave of his time
Gave no money	Paid for all his needs
Offered no empathy	Had pity on the man
Hands off	Personally tended to the wounds
Travel inconvenience	Used his own donkey to carry the man
Interfered with religious duties/ritual cleanliness	No religious interference
Insecure	Secure

If true security, according to Jesus, looks more like the Samaritan than like the priest and the Levite, then we may have to reorient the way we respond to what we see in our neighbourhoods. We may need to rethink what security means. Author Mark Labberton says that the American Dream is a paradigm that's all about "doing everything necessary or possible to make life secure."[52] We work 40-80 hours a week to ensure every part of our lives is secure. Not only does this buy us the things we want in order to feel secure, but we need to keep up our busy pace in order to maintain the system we have created. For some, the system of security we maintain might be in our stuff, our bank accounts, our pleasures, our social network, our education, or travel experiences. We are set on making the world around us secure from the beginning, and unless we have reason to believe differently, our own personal security and wellbeing will always remain the centre of our attention and affection.

But security is something we all strive for. How could we dare suggest otherwise? Protecting what is yours, building a safety net, keeping yourself out of trouble, aren't these all noble things? Isn't life full of enough trouble? In some deep sense, you may be afraid that if you let your guard down for a moment you'll just be letting in more challenges, more frustrations, and more insecurity. Shouldn't your church, your neighbourhood, your family, God, and this book all be helping you to secure a good life for yourself and your family?

These concerns are at the heart of Jesus' picture of security: it rests with God, not with the ability of the person to provide it for themselves. The priest and the Levite in Jesus' story were probably all rehearsing that same monologue - keep your head down, hold on to what you have, and get through the day. For Jesus, this did not represent the most secure path. In God's economy, holding on to what you have may result in losing it all. In Matthew 16:25 Jesus says, "If you try to hang on to your life, you will lose it. But if you give up your life for my sake, you will save it." And perhaps that's why the Samaritan makes the right choice. He did not seek merely his own way, but was lauded for living into God's work around him. By seeing the world through God's eyes and trusting in God's provision of security and resources, the Samaritan fulfills Christ's call to "love your neighbour as yourself" (Mark 12:31).

When we have our head down, working on our own security system, we cannot see what is around us. For the priest and the Levite, the man on the side of the road was a minor distraction until they snapped back to their 'reality' of self-security. The same thing is true for us. When we are so focused on our 50-hour work week and all the preparations needed to secure our world, we cannot see our neighbours, hear their stories, point to the places where God is at work in their lives, or sense where God is leading them and us. Our narrow focus on our own wellbeing leaves us with no focus on the beautiful things God is doing all around us. The pursuit of our security leaves the world around us vulnerable and uncared for.

Keystone people and those who are awake to beauty and are able to turn their gaze away from their own security and find out how God is creating another kind of security in the neighbourhoods that they call home. As people who seek to bless the neighbourhood we must become people who see the need, and see God working to address that need. Mark Labberton refers to this as the need for renewed 'sight-lines.' He says, "Our vision is not only a limited frame; it's biased. [We see] from the perch of our own self-interest. Our sight-lines are by no means neutral or comprehensive."[53]

If our 'sight-lines' are limited, and we often do not see our neighbourhood as God does, then how are we able to respond well? How do we turn our focus from ourselves and onto what God is doing? How does our security become a secondary priority to the trusting relationship we have with God when we connect with our neighbours? The answer for this lies in our deepest understanding of the Father's love and provision for us. It is only in taking on the eyes of the Father for a broken world that we gain new sight-lines and a heart of compassion.

Real Security

I started to occasionally leave the doors on our house unlocked a few years ago. It was risky, for sure. Anyone could have just walked into our home and walked off with our slow cooker or our cleaning supplies. It could have all been gone in an instant. But the story didn't happen that way. We still have our stuff, but something inside of us started to change. The revolutionary act of not locking our doors has created a small but profound change of heart in us. We see our security differently.

I discovered something about myself every time I locked my front door. I found that I was rehearsing a pattern of selfish security: everything inside is mine. It's mine to keep safe and protect. It's mine to use and share only on my terms. Similarly, I was subtly reinforcing a belief that the people around me are a threat to my stuff, untrustworthy and likely to take advantage of me. If not today, then tomorrow. When I locked the door I was keeping my stuff in and keeping the baddies out. So we decided to do an experiment. I discovered that when we did not lock our door, even as a one-time (and only one-time) careful experiment, this radical gesture reminded us that the stuff inside was not ours to hold on to so tightly, and that the people outside were not enemies scheming our downfall.

I'm not saying this prescriptively, but rather descriptively. When we lock the door it reinforces the story that our life's goal is to get, maintain, and secure our stuff. But when we don't lock the door, even once, it is a powerful gesture that reminds us that our life's goal is to participate with God, living generously, openly, welcoming others in, and sharing life in the same way the Father lovingly shares his life with us. The act of unlocking your door is more about a statement you wish to make in your own heart, a tangible reminder of God's security which shields us and the radical life of hospitality that Christians are called to live.

For you, the experiment might not be to unlock your door. But consider, what are some other ways you can address self-focused security in your own life? How can you experiment with ways of putting greater trust in God and building a culture of trust in your own neighbourhood?

Jesus did one thing that each of us can do. He trusted the Father's ability and willingness to give security to his children. Over and over again Jesus tells his disciples not to be afraid, that God will provide for them, and he encourages their baby steps when they experiment to push through their own insecurities and trust in God. In fact, the early church grew and impacted the world around them when they lived generously with their possessions, took in orphaned babies, or gave of their time to make their neighbourhoods better places. Christians had a reputation for caring not only for their own, but for non-Christians as well. This was the ethos of the early church because they saw and experienced the same thing that Jesus did - a growing trust and love for the Father. When God's people truly grasp the depth of God's capacity to provide security and care for a security-starved world, we begin to live with an entirely new perspective and impetus for living. It's not about us anymore. The pressure is off to try to save ourselves. As Eugene Peterson's *The Message* version of 1 Peter 5:7 puts it, "Live carefree before God; he is most careful with you."

If we continue to live as though our own security is in our hands, we will miss some of the most vital experiences of our lives. By stepping out from behind the walls of safety, we begin to see those places where God is performing miracles, providing for needs, rescuing, rebuilding, joy-infusing, and creating beauty. You begin to see your neighbourhood as God does.

Allies

My wife, Kelly, served as a medical relief worker in Haiti and Brazil, but some of her best stories came from the year she spent working with farmers in Zambia. She was staying in a rented home with a beautiful guava tree in the garden. As the season changed, her yard blossomed into life and soon fruit was hanging heavily from the branches. One day she noticed that guavas were disappearing from her guava tree. It didn't take long for her to discover why. A small group of young boys were sneaking into the yard, stealing from her tree and then running off. So one day she waited for the little opportunists to come around and she intercepted them just as they were about to take some more fruit. She called them all over, and with heads hanging down they knew the gig was up.

But my wife was more clever and more gracious than they knew. She said, "Boys, I need your help. Someone has been stealing from my guava tree. Can you believe it?" The little pilferers were speechless. "I'd like to hire all of you to be my guava tree guards," she went on, "If you guard my guava tree from thieves, I'll repay you by letting you take as many guavas as you need. What do you think? Do we have a deal?" The boys were shocked, and then elated. They just landed a prestigious security job that paid in delicious guavas! Soon the group of boys organized themselves into shifts to guard the tree around the clock from the 'yet-to-be-found' guava thieves. All season long the boys would report that the garden was safe and all the boys enjoyed their fill of well-earned fruit. It was funny, gracious, and genius.

From thieves to allies, it is amazing what a thoughtful gesture of kindness can do. My wife had the ability to see beyond these young boys' thieving activities and recognize that they had the capacity to do something meaningful. What she did changed the way those boys related to the world around them. When she made these boys her allies, when she sided with them, she opened the door to relationship. No longer were they slinking around in the dark, they became people she knew by name and welcomed every day. Instead of living with the fear that their guava-stealing might move to larger crimes, my wife was able to live with a sense of comfort knowing that while she was away a team of boys had a protective eye on her home.

An ally is someone whom you look out for and who you trust with your own well-being. We talk about allied nations who partner together for a higher cause or a common purpose, but what would it look like for us to be allies to our neighbours?

A neighbourhood of allies is a rare and powerful thing. Often most people on a street do not know their neighbours, let alone work together with them out of trust and kindness. It is enticing to think of my city as a place where neighbours become allies and where residents become partners. If guava thieves can become dedicated guava security guards because of a moment of kindness, imagine what our neighbourhoods could look like if we saw the people on our street as our own allies, friends, and partners.

A renewed imagination for God's work in our neighbourhood reorients our lives to a whole new way of seeing those around us. As we live open-handed lives God will begin to unclench our hold on our security and free us to embrace again.

Making the Invisible Visible: Security

Our security systems are built into us from childhood as we're taught to avoid strangers and stay safely on our side of the fence. Over time those safety systems can turn against God's work in our lives as we avoid our neighbours and the interactions we might be having. When we look around ourselves and see that the world is actually longing for connections, and when we are able to see beyond our own self-security, we may discover that Jesus was onto something when he called us to love our neighbours. When we step outside of ourselves and engage with others, we may actually end up leading a happier and more fulfilling life. The command to love our neighbours is as much an invitation to freedom and joy for ourselves as it is for bringing life to the neighbourhoods where we live. Stepping into God's security and into the lives of others requires some prayerful self-reflection in order to shine a light on those places where we feel most safe. To do this, we start with an experiment.

1. Security system profile: Do you do everything necessary or possible to make life secure? Write down the top ten things in your life that make you feel safe, hopeful, and happy. Keep that list with you for a couple of days and review it when you have the chance. Think about the story that Jesus told of the Good Samaritan and ask yourself whether your security system profile opens your life to others or keeps you 'safe' from others. Think about what you could change to allow you to give up your safety in the ways that the Good Samaritan did.

2. Fulfilling conversations: A study was done by some behavioural scientists a few years ago. They asked subway commuters to break all the rules. Typically,

the social rule on public transit is avert your gaze, look at your smart-phone, and stay quiet. But these scientists found that most people on public transit were unhappy. They hated their commute. So the scientists asked a few people if they would have a conversation with a stranger. The result was simple "By the end of the train ride, commuters who talked to a stranger reported having a more positive experience than those who had sat in solitude." But the experiment went further than that. Before each participant went to talk to a stranger, most participants predicted that they would have a negative experience. They predicted that they would be happier if they just sat on their own, quietly, like everyone else. However, the behavioural scientist found that nearly 99 per cent of the people who spoke to strangers had a very positive experience. The open connections also turned out to be contagious. They found that "far from annoying people by violating their personal bubbles, reaching out to strangers may improve their day, too."[54] The belief that we are happier when we are alone, segregated, and quiet, and that all those around us are also happier in their disconnected state, is actually proving to be a lie. Studies like these show that nearly all people walk away from a conversation with a stranger with good feelings. Ask yourself this: If I could engage in an activity that had a 99 per cent chance of making me happier and more fulfilled, would I take it? If I lived a life that welcomed others into my world, do I predict that it would be a good or bad experience? Am I a good predictor of what really makes me happy? 3. Where does my help come from? The Bible is rich with language that releases our imaginations to see our security in new ways. Read Psalm 121 and reflect on how God may be realigning your security system as you seek to live into the neighbourhood where you live, and that God loves.

Psalm 121
A song for pilgrims ascending to Jerusalem.
1 I look up to the mountains—
 does my help come from there?
2 My help comes from the Lord,
 who made heaven and earth!
3 He will not let you stumble;
 the one who watches over you will not slumber.

4 Indeed, he who watches over Israel
 never slumbers or sleeps.
5 The Lord himself watches over you!
 The Lord stands beside you as your protective shade.
6 The sun will not harm you by day,
 nor the moon at night.
7 The Lord keeps you from all harm
 and watches over your life.
8 The Lord keeps watch over you as you come and go,
 both now and forever.

Boring

Wonderfully Boring

"The hum of bees is the voice of the garden, a sound that lends new meaning to the flowers and the silence"
- Elizabeth Lawrence[55]

Boring is good. Boring is creative. Boring is wonderfully beautiful. And boring is a very hard sell.

Who writes a chapter celebrating boredom, anyway?

As we seek to shape our imaginations to see God's work unfolding in our neighbourhoods, then boredom becomes a powerful posture that changes how we live and thrive in the places we live.

Recently my wife and I went to a *Cirque du Soleil* show. From the start to the end, it was pure sugar for the senses, a rush of colours, live music, super-human feats of acrobatic beauty and athleticism, all topped off with a whip-cream dollop of mystery and surprise. It was wonderful! The best forms of entertainment take spectators to other places. They delight and enthral. *Cirque du Soleil* did all this for me.

When the performance was over we sat in our seats as the audience cleared out, not really wanting it to be over. After 15 minutes the cold fluorescent lights flickered on and the mystery vanished as the stagehands dressed in black, repositioned the props and adjusted the spider's web of cables and pulleys. On our slow walk out I took some time to speak with the crew. They had none of the excitement that I had and one of them told me how he was thinking about finding work elsewhere. Frankly, he looked tired.

On the drive home that evening we were still buzzing with enthusiasm. I turned onto our quiet street. The street lights were the same dull yellow, we saw the usual shadows of families watching TV in their living rooms, and my own home was dark and, well, comparatively boring.

Boring, it seems, is the natural default position for most of our lives. We eat, we work, we come, we go. Yet our understanding of boring may be the starting place for a new way of seeing the world around us. Instead of fixating our imaginations on the next entertaining circus act we can find, maybe we should focus our imagination more deeply on those boring things around us.

Here's why: A study was done by Dr. Sandi Mann into the value of boredom for creativity. She discovered that certain kinds of boredom lead to daydreaming, and that daydreaming actually increases the mind's ability to come up with new ideas. She found that the longer researchers engaged their subjects in thoroughly boring circumstances, their ability to come up with new ideas or solutions increased.[56] Boredom leads to creativity. In a measurable sense, boredom can be good for our thinking and ability to engage new ideas which then allow for true creativity.

Similarly, Dr. Teresa Belton with the University of East Anglia said that the lack of things to do spurred her "to talk to people she would not otherwise have engaged with and to try activities she would not, under other circumstances, have experienced, such as talking to elderly neighbours and learning to bake cakes."[57] In the pursuit of creative productivity it has been long assumed that more activity, input, discussion, dialogue, projects, social media engagement - more 'doing' - would lead to better results for our companies, churches, or neighbourhoods. However it may be that moments of intentional input-free boredom may be just the thing we need to inspire healthy creativity and engagement.

On most days our neighbourhoods do not play host to festivals, fairs, or concerts. More likely our streets and parks are quiet places where people simply walk, sit, and relax. Our neighbourhoods are naturally quite boring. Even now, outside my window, a neighbour is watching his grandkids wobble their bikes back and forth along our street. The thrill of a kid on training wheels is a far cry from the fantastical world of *Cirque du Soleil*, but the impact that boring places and quiet settings bring to those who know their value is profound.

To some, 'boring' might be an overstated term. Perhaps 'calm' or 'restful' or 'spiritual' may seem more appropriate. However, those meaningful moments when God works in our lives are seldom seen as obviously spiritual. There is this false sense that somehow, in a moment of ethereal awakening, we will always clearly see God's hand at work in our midst. Often it is only after the fact that we recognize the presence of God having been at play during a banal conversation or encounter. In this sense, 'boring' is precisely the word that we should use. To accept that God is fully engaged in the tedious, in the dull, in the monotonous, or in the uninteresting moments of our lives is a pivotal step in coming to a place of living into what God is doing. God works in boring places at boring times, and perhaps God is calling us to be present in those places and times so that we might enjoy his presence there.

Neighbours with a renewed imagination for their neighbourhood need to be those who are willing to be where the *in*-action might be. In doing so, we may find that we are precisely where God is at work in unexpected and surprising ways.

David, the King after God's own heart, seemed to have led anything but a boring life. He fought a giant, played music, fought in battles, and was chased across hills and valleys by a mad king before becoming the king himself. For such a storied life and journey of faith, you would not be faulted to think that King David must have written songs of praise lauding intense action-filled spirituality. Yet David sings in Psalm 40 about how he "waited patiently for the Lord." He goes on to celebrate all the wonderful things God has done and how as a result "many will ... put their trust in the Lord."[58] David frequently turned the reader's attention towards God. He learned this posture of waiting and trusting in God from his time sleeping under the stars, looking after his sheep, or hiding in a cave. His own journey of faith grew during times of monotonous seasons in the wilderness. He saw and met God in the boredom and celebrated the trust relationship he had with God.

The Apostle Paul writes to the Galatians about the fruit of the Holy Spirit and settles on a list, which, at first glance, is rather boring. He says, "The Holy Spirit produces this kind of fruit in our lives: love, joy, peace, patience, kindness, goodness, faithfulness, gentleness, and self-control. There is no law against these things!"[59] It's not macho. Not particularly adventurous. There is very little that's initially exciting about a small act of kindness. A loving gesture or pause to offer gentle care will never measure up in any hierarchy of mind-melting entertainment. Yet the neighbour who exhibits the fruit of the Holy Spirit is one who makes room for these boring moments.

Moments of waiting and listening lead to moments of laughter and care. Those attentive to the Holy Spirit and those being shaped by Jesus's character are positioned in such a way that they embrace the boring because they know that this is where God is at work. A new longing for kindness and gentleness is shaped in our imaginations when we stop to see the world through these new spiritual lenses.

We face a challenge. Boredom has become something we aim to avoid at every turn. With smartphones always at the ready to provide a steady distraction, we're able to avoid boredom at all times. Jonny Smallwood, professor of cognitive neuroscience at the University of York says, "What smartphones allow us to do is get rid of boredom in a very direct way because we can play games, phone people, we can check the Internet. It takes away the boredom, but it also denies us the chance to see and learn about where we truly are in terms of our goals."[60] As we try to avoid boredom we risk stepping right past those moments of creative engagement with those around us. We risk failing to see the kids and their grandpa playing on the street or the quiet family who lives on the corner. In fact the most important details of God's work in our neighbourhoods could be completely off our radar if we do not position ourselves to see them. Often the only way we can see what is happening around us is if we embrace boredom.

But we do not long for just any kind of boredom, as though we are looking for tedious moments of disconnect from the world around us. When good ideas strike us in the shower, it's because these are the moments when we are not at work, not trying to focus, not attempting to perform in any way. These are moments when we are alone with our thoughts and quite unable to achieve very much. The daily routine of getting ready in the morning is, frankly, rather boring. Researchers say it is no surprise that these kind of boredom moments actually do produce the 'ah-ha' thoughts that fill our imaginations and open our eyes to see the world around us.

Weakness, boredom, and performance-less moments are those where God also reminds us of his love and grace for us. Through Jesus we are the recipients of the Father's unrelenting grace and love. We are called to see the world through God's eyes, and with his heart. Yet when we pursue unrelenting entertainment, closing off those times of boredom, weakness, and frailty, we may miss those places where God is reminding us that we belong to him. We may fail to see that God is capable of more than all we can imagine because our capacity to imagine is hampered. By embracing the beauty of boredom, we become people who can truly see God at work. And when we see God at work, it becomes anything but boring.

Hygge

My life's on the line before God, my Lord,
waiting and watching till morning,
waiting and watching till morning.
-Psalm 130:5-6 *(The Message)*

I remember when my then-two-year-old learned a particular new word. She woke up at 7:00 am and pointed outside saying, 'Dark! Dark!' I leaned over her crib, picked her up and quietly told her that she's a Canadian and that 'dark,' 'cold,' and 'snow' are words that she'll be using quite a bit over the next few months. Our garden and apiary, which used to be bathed in sunlight, are under a long shadow that time of year. It is amazing to think that by the time the shortest day of the year comes around, on December 21st, our days will have eight-and-a-half fewer hours of daylight than we had in June.

Welcome to winter in Alberta.

For many, winter is dark on other levels, too. For some this time of year means increased isolation from friends, the frustration of feeling confined indoors, and the potential for seasonal depression. Add to that a post-Christmas credit card bill and all of this cold and gloom might leave us thinking that getting on the next plane to Mexico is the only way to find relief. Winter darkness is a struggle against boredom as we wait until the light and warmth visits us again. However a researcher with the University of Tromsø, Norway, and Stanford University has found that not all northern cultures respond negatively to the cold and dark months of winter. Kari Leibowitz discovered that "in Tromsø, the Polar Night seemed to hold its own unique opportunities for mental and emotional flourishing."[61] Instead of being a place of dark sorrow, the people of Norway have practiced an approach to becoming people of life. Their winter-time postures and practices not only help them endure nearly total darkness, but they have found ways of ensuring that everyone in their community makes it through together.

The Norwegians have a word that speaks to getting through the winter: 'koselig.' There is no easy English equivalent for, it but the closest might be akin to cozy, welcoming, relaxed, tranquil, homey, and friendly. It is the feeling of a warm fire, hot cocoa, the perfect blanket, and good food. But even more than that, it is the sense of getting cozy with others. Researchers are discovering that during the darkest months of the year, many Norwegians are creating special times with friends, huddled around a fire, with the lights down low, and finding happiness in the midst of darkness.

Similarly, the Danes use the word, 'hygge.' Pronounced 'heurgha' (say it as though you are clearing your throat, I'm told), the word is equally significant. Jeppe Trolle Linnet defines 'hygge' as a "safe habitat; the experience of comfort and joy ... a caring connotation ... behaviour that other people find easy to get along with, one that soothes them and builds trust."[62] Hygge, while also a celebration of coziness and togetherness, adds an element of gratitude. Being grateful for these moments and experiences with others, with hot drinks and blazing fires, is what makes this time of year so meaningful. Additionally, 'hygge' has become a time when friends resist talking about divisive topics of conversation and they do not talk as a prelude to getting things done. Danes who adopt this posture believe that more 'stuff' isn't needed to find happiness during these long, dark days, but instead the focus is on creating intentional welcoming spaces to gather with others.

All of this might sound a little too fuzzy-touchy-feely for some. But consider that Denmark and Norway are often ranked among the happiest countries in the world. It is believed that a strong focus on our emotional wellbeing and the importance of friendships, along with a hot cup of tea and a cozy setting, might just be what the doctor ordered for the winter-blahs. As a result, many people take great pride in truly embracing the ethos and activity of gathering with others and enjoying some downtime.

In some respects, '*hygge*' helps us embrace boredom. It is not a cure, but instead a renewing of our imaginations to see our circumstances differently. In the search for a response to boredom, some turn up the volume or the intensity of their favourite diversion. Yet it has been my experience that you can be in a room full of noise, and still feel disconnected and bored. '*Hygge*,' then, allows us to embrace the boredom by welcoming us to step into quiet moments with others, guided by the hope of creating peace.

In our own neighbourhoods we have an opportunity to turn cookie cutter rows of homes, or uninspiring streets and apartment blocks into so much more. As we adjust our perspective to see light in the darkness, we become those people who carve out hope and life shared with others in the places where we live. Boredom, through this lens, becomes an opportunity for mid-winter delight.

Whether you live in a dark northern climate or not, think about ways that you might create '*koselig*' or '*hygge*' practices in your own life and home. Find ways to gather with others, set a warm atmosphere, resist the urge to be productive or entertained, and enjoy the quiet company of others. You may find that the people around you become the light you need to make it through a dark and cold season.

The Garden and the Pilcrow

"This is how we make important changes- barely, poorly, slowly."
-Anne Lamott[63]

When gardens thrive, you know it. You can smell the aroma of sweet peas, you can see the lively buds and blossoms, you can feel the thick green grass between your toes, and here and there you can hear the buzz of bees and the chirping of song birds. It might take a seasoned green thumb to explain exactly how a garden becomes healthy, but anyone can tell if a garden is thriving or not.

Knowing when our city or neighbourhood is thriving might be a bigger challenge. How do we measure vitality in our neighbourhoods? At first glance, almost every neighbourhood looks the same, even boring. They have houses, cars might be coming and going, there may be buildings and parks dotted throughout. Yet people instinctively know when their community is thriving or not.

Recently I was visiting another Alberta community. I spent some time speaking with local residents. It became clear to me that they felt their neighbourhood was not thriving. They told me about how people did not connect, how community groups were closing down. I left with a sense that something had knocked the wind out of them. Although they could not put their finger on what was missing from their community, they knew that their neighbourhood was not thriving.

Here is a gardening secret. The trick to gardening is "attentive faithfulness." You will not find this term in gardening books, but all the best gardeners walk through their gardens with this posture. Here is what it looks like: firstly, they pay attention to their garden, the soil, the weather, and their seeds. They study the ground and the sun and find the very best places to plant. Their keen eyes see gardens as more than a jumble of plants but as a thriving, dynamic, living world. Gardeners are masters of seeing the unseen, of paying attention to the tiny clues around them.

Secondly, gardeners are faithful. They stick it out for the whole season, year after year. When others have called it a day, gardeners are putting on their boots and getting their hands dirty. They create watering schedules and know when to move tender potted plants from the safety of the kitchen window out into the garden. They respond to their garden and, in a sense, grow with it. When a problem comes up, the best gardeners don't just cut down a bush or spray chemicals over their garden, they work first to understand it. Then they take all that they have seen and find creative solutions. Under the care of an attentive and faithful gardener, life emerges.

This inherent posture of the best gardeners is also the secret to a healthy, thriving neighbourhood. Those with a renewed imagination for their neighbourhoods are those who stand with a posture of "attentive faithfulness" to the world around them. They pay attention to the people, the kids, the dog park, and the community groups. They study the challenges and look for those little corners where good things are happening. They have eyes to see their city as more than boring rows of houses but as a dynamic, complex, and beautiful community worth investing in. Neighbourhood enthusiasts are also those who are faithful. They find ways to encourage community, gather people, and cheer on goodness. When they see a chance to bring life, they work together with others to make their neighbourhood thrive.

At the hands of attentive and faithful people, neighbourhoods can thrive. And when a city thrives, you know it. The gardener, like the neighbourhood builder, is more than the sideline-cheerleading-champion of nostalgic or sentimental goodness. Rather, they become pivotal in changing the story.

The faithfully attentive become the neighbourhood pilcrow.

A pilcrow is an ancient written symbol. Today it is largely hidden, but it used to be found everywhere. It looks like this:

Pilcrows were used by scribes to show a break in a thought or an idea, closing off one idea and starting another. Scribes had commas, periods, and other notations, but they needed to create a way of beginning a new paragraph. Enter the pilcrow. For centuries, it served the purpose of helping readers mentally switch gears. One symbol turned the corner, shifted thought, and advanced the story. The pilcrow is still with us, but it's hidden in our word processors. In your word processor, click "Show invisibles" and you'll see the pilcrow all over. It is there, ending one idea and showing the start of another.

Today, pilcrow neighbours are those who see the invisible in their neighbourhoods and choose to nurture and foster new directions and potential within them. In our persistent and often uncelebrated posture of care in the face of quiet uneventful rhythms of ordinary neighbourhood life, we are invited to indicate a new way. We turn our neighbourhoods towards fresh ideas, new metaphors, and hopeful stories. Our attentive faithfulness becomes more than a waiting game; it produces an active sense of breaking the cycles of loneliness, despair, and selfishness by conceptualizing - and even realizing - what is possible. Neighbours have the power to step into the boredom they experience and set a new direction of purpose and hope.

These images of the garden and the pilcrow may perhaps seem odd, but we need surprising new lenses through which to see the humdrum daily comings and goings of our neighbourhood. We need to boldly embrace boredom as the start of a renewed imagination, primed for creativity. We need to be those who create warmth and safety in the midst of darkness. All around us we need to see more than just the typical suburban houses or box stores or the nameless masses we share the bus with on our way to work. In the boring places is a beautiful beginning where life is waiting to be fostered and nurtured, and it begins with a pilcrow and a few people willing to become faithfully attentive to their neighbourhood.

What we need

Well, you've made it through, quite literally, the most boring chapter in this book. But boredom is something we deeply need.

Being a beekeeper can get boring.

Being a pastor can get boring.

Being me - a neighbour, husband, father, taxpayer, grocery-shopping, lawn-mowing writer - can all be boring.

Yet I am learning that boredom is often what we need to begin to see anew. The goal and destination of my life is to join with God in what God is doing in the places where I live and work, in the places where I love and laugh and cry. Sometimes the journey to this goal begins in the quiet, unassuming places right before me. If there is one thing I have learned, it is that Jesus is standing right there before me too. Up to his knees in it, delighting in my neighbourhood, and inviting me to join in.

Will you step in?

Making the Invisible Visible: Boring

You might not be afraid of the boogeyman, but you may be afraid of boredom. We are driven to fill every moment of our day with an endless stream of entertainment, news, social connections, hobbies, or projects. When we realize that we are boredom-adverse, we may also come to see that we are in fact limiting our ability to simply stop, watch, listen, and be present to what God is doing in our neighbourhood. We are being invited to become those who can are faithfully attentive long enough to turn the story in a new direction. These practices and postures offer an entry point to help you embrace moments of boredom and begin to reshape the ways you think about those around you.

1. From screen time to downtime: Take stock of how often you turn to your computer, TV, or smartphone every time you feel bored. Here are some ways of gauging how readily you turn to your phone whenever you have a moment. First, consider moving your phone away from your body for a week. Keep it nearby when an important call comes in, but consider how much your screen has become an extension of your body, an easy go-to solution for moments of boredom. Second, reset how your smartphone communicates with you. Does it need to notify you of every text and message, or can those wait? By lowering your phone's ability to infringe on downtime, you free up your mind's ability to focus on the present moment and place. Thirdly, consider

making a category of time that may allow for boredom. The creative result of time spent doing 'nothing' may actually produce more imagination than time spent feeding on the creative works of others.

2. Make people wait: I heard a story of a man who made no time for others during a short while every morning, unless it was an emergency. He created this space so that he could think, wait, reflect, pray, hope, and dream. He found this time of boredom set him in such a posture that he was present for others the rest of the day. In an age of instant access and demand for immediate response to emails and texts, it is countercultural to make others wait. However, as we limit our need to respond impulsively, we actually make more room to care well for others. As Pope Francis once said to his friends, "The first answer that comes to me is usually wrong."[64] Making room allows for moments of boredom to produce the kinds of responses that could bring life and which better reflect what God is doing in that moment.

3. Notice the lack of boredom: Go to the local coffee shop, order a drink, and just sit and wait. Notice how others refuse to be bored. Work, socializing, and smartphones dominate the space. Reflect. Sense your own urgency to fill your own time. Now consider how those moments of boredom have in fact created a new direction for your own thinking and motivation.

4. Invite: Ask God to join you in a boredom moment. Invite God to sit with you in a wordless time of rest. Consider that God is not put off by your lack of prayer but enjoys sitting with you. Reflect on how times of boredom with God can actually shape the way you trust God and rely on God's provision for you.

5. Sit and watch the bees.

Taste of Place

Honey Tasting

Every summer I host a neighbourhood honey-tasting event in my backyard for our community, and tickets are bought up right away. There's something alluring about such an event. It is a feast for the senses - and the imagination. Over time it has also become a great way to connect with others. I've often said that you can't go wrong when you fill a house with garden, beekeeping, and neighbourhood enthusiasts. It makes for a wonderful evening.

Throughout the year I collect honey from around the world to showcase, along with a few bottles of mead and lots of good food. Not only does honey hold the distinction of being the only food made by insects and consumed by humans, but it carries the astonishing fingerprint of the land where it came from. Honey from the Bugaboo mountains in British Columbia comes from one of the highest-altitude apiaries in Canada, and the Jubilee Mountain Apiary offers honey with notes of pine tree and mountain flowers. I was given a small jar of honey from Laos with a little tag on it saying, "Taste Laos! This Lao honey is hunted by honey hunters in the Lao jungle. ...This is exactly the taste of the jungle of Laos." Even my own honey from year to year, captures the taste of my neighbourhood; the trees and flowers which grow in its backyards shape the flavour, and the nearby cultivated crops of canola or hay make my flavour-profile unique in all the world. Each taste of honey tells a story of the place where it came from, and my honey-tasting event is truly a 'taste of place' and a window into the living world around me.

Several years ago I had a chance to visit a beekeeping research facility in Nairobi, Kenya, and buy some honey from the beekeepers in that region. There the honey is dark and tastes something like molasses. The bees visit tropical plants, and the strong flavours of the nectar they collect shapes the flavour profile of their honey. While I was there, I also had a chance to let the beekeepers taste Canadian honey. While I found their honey too strong, they thought my honey was too weak. There we were, beekeepers from opposite sides of the globe, laughing like old friends at the odd taste of each other's honey. We each realized the ways in which the places we live shape our palates and appreciation for the honey we know and have come to love.

Not only does honey give a taste of place, but some honey tells a deeper story. Honey from Lebanon comes from bees who sometimes cross the border into Israel to collect nectar from trees growing there, and it has a distinct orange-blossom taste. Honey bees from Israel travel north of the border into war-torn Syria. While human borders limit access between countries, honey bees are becoming a symbol of peace who know no borders. The honey they produce is shared around the world; it is a reminder of conflict and a longing for peace. Tasting this Lebanese honey offers a moment to reflect. It is quite profound.

In fact, there is more going on at a neighbourhood honey-tasting event than we may see. We are experiencing the world through our taste buds and through the experiences of insects around the world. Honey captures the flavours of flowers long gone and opens a window into our imagination. When we taste honey from a different place, we are compelled to reflect on our own homes, imagining the impact that our own gardens have on the taste of the honey we share together. Could my apple tree have affected this honey? What about the catmint we have growing in the front flower bed? The dynamic layers of our neighbourhoods affect the taste of the honey being produced. Some parts of the world are nectar deserts, some produce ambrosia. What would honey from your neighbourhood taste like? What is the taste of your place?

About one Saturday a month in the summer I set up a little honey booth on our front porch and put the word out on Chestermere social media. People can stop by, put a few dollars in the 'honey money' jar, and leave with a big jar of amber honey, warmed by the afternoon sun. Within a few hours the dozen or so jars I put out are gone. It is a fun little exercise in trust, sharing the bounty. Often I get to bump into the neighbours as they come and go. The best part of those Saturdays are the notes I get from those who taste the honey. Usually it's a variation of, "This is nothing like the stuff we get at the store. It's delicious."

For many people, the honey they've tasted is from a big box store. Much of that honey comes from honey bees, but here's the interesting thing: these bees do not make their honey in the way you would expect. Much of the 'Canada Grade A Honey' that is found on some store shelves is a blend of cheap honey from a variety of countries. In some countries, and even here in Canada, many beekeepers do not expect their bees to gather flower nectar to produce their honey. In fact, many commercial apiaries are simply too far away from any significant source of nectar to produce any reasonable amount of honey. So how do they produce honey at all? Often these producers will feed their honey bees some form of sugar water or corn syrup - and by the truckload. Special feeding barrels full of this liquid are consumed by the bees and converted into honey. This 'honey' is collected from the hives and shipped to Canada to be sold cheaply at many grocery stores.

Similarly, in places were pollen might be scarce, industrial bee operations may also feed their bees artificial pollen patties. It's possible that bees in some countries may spend their whole lives eating little more than artificial pollen and artificial nectar in the form of sugar water. Is the product you buy in the local grocery store still honey? Well, it does come from bees. Yet it may contain only trace amounts of real flower nectar. For those who buy cheap honey, they are often pleasantly surprised when they taste local, 'real' honey for the first time. It's magical.

The word we sometimes use to describe the specific qualities of local honey is "terroir." This is an old French term that reflects the "taste of place." It refers to all the factors that make honey taste the way it does. From the altitude of the beehives, to the kind of flora to which the bees have access, terroir is a helpful way of understanding the complex qualities of honey. Other factors such as humidity, geography, climate, and even microorganisms native to some parts of the world will all affect the 'terroir' of honey. For foodies, this element of 'terroir' is especially intriguing. Suddenly a simple jar of honey may become a fascinating journey into the specific history, weather, and botany of apiaries in farflung countries.

As I taste the world through jars of honey and reflect on the taste of my own neighbourhood, I have begun to wonder: does my neighbourhood have 'terroir' of another, deeper kind? Do I have the imagination to see God's hand at work shaping the unique qualities of beauty and hope, life and love, in my own community and along my street? Does Rainbow Falls, Chestermere, Alberta, Canada, have a kind of flavour that makes it unique in all the world?

In many ways, my neighbourhood is a mix of suburban houses, with cars and trucks lining the streets. Families from different backgrounds come and go, and in some ways anyone could pass through and never really reflect on what would make this neighbourhood unique. I am starting to see that in the same way an apple tree or catmint could subtly contribute to the flavour profile of my honey, there is some kind of beautiful potential built into my neighbourhood. Individuals and families have before them a chance to change the taste of their place.

Rainbow Falls, whether we know it or not, has terroir.

Lettera 22

I find the best way to change the 'taste of place' is through the subtle and beautiful acts that make good things come to life. Kind words, presence, attentiveness, and courage are some ingredients in the spice cabinet of those hoping to season the places where they live. Neighbourhoods change, not through a petition or program, but through the ongoing work that comes from people who see their neighbourhood with new eyes. Small, careful, and subtle. One way that I have found to change the taste of my place is to turn to the ancient art of letter-writing.

As a pastor I've made it a practice to write letters to people. I used to write cards by hand, but that changed when I bought a used Lettera 22 typewriter. It's old, and a bit finicky, but oddly satisfying. When I meet new people, or want to encourage a friend, there is something good that happens when I pull down my typewriter and take it out of the case. It takes a few minutes to set up, find a nice sheet of small typewriter paper, and adjust the ribbon. I take that time to think about what I want to write, how I want to convey my thoughts. Then, clack, clack, clack, I write. It's nothing like writing a column, email, tweet, or essay. It's slow, methodical, and strangely raw. Typewriters have no 'backspace' or way of correcting mistakes. If I make an error, it stays on the sheet, perhaps crossed out, but there nonetheless. Typing takes time and I find myself getting to the point of what I want to convey. Maybe, "thanks for being my neighbour" is all I need to say sometimes.

The real magic comes from sending the letter in the mail. In a world of emails and junk mail, a personally written letter sent with intentionality is a powerful and countercultural gesture. My typewriter a stack of simple typewriter paper, and some stamps have transformed relationships and conversations. Sending letters or cards might seem like a grandmotherly kind of activity, right there along with crochet or 1,000-piece puzzles. I've found that a moment spent sending a letter, expressing my thoughts in simple and kind ways can shape the way I see others.

Years ago I painted portraits of people in our church congregation. It is a project that turned into something larger. I would simply sit down with some watercolour paints and a blank piece of paper, and create. It was slow work, each painting would take days or weeks. But as I would sit and paint I would find myself praying, almost like sitting with the person in real life. I was asking God to bless them, I would wonder what God was doing in their lives, and I would just be present to God's nudging in my own heart. It was a unique experience in my life, and I don't think I've ever prayed so much for other people as I did when I was painting their portraits. It was a function, I believe, of simply being present and patient with them before God.

When I'm in my office clacking away on my old, little, blue typewriter I find myself entering a similar place of prayer for the people I am writing to. The slow work of writing this way allows me a moment to listen, reflect, and allow God space to speak. My Lettera 22 typewriter is a little altar of prayer.

A few years ago I wrote to Eugene Peterson with my little typewriter. He is a voice of wisdom for pastors, and his books have taught me to reflect about the pace and posture of my life as a pastor and neighbour. By slowing down and living intentionally with the people and place where God has brought me, I'm more likely to see and participate in what God is already doing all around me. Eugene Peterson has long since been retired, and I heard he was living somewhat off the grid. Or at the very least, he wasn't checking his Twitter or Facebook feeds like the rest of us. So I pulled down my typewriter and wrote him the old-fashioned way. I had been thinking a lot about what it means to love my neighbours, slowly, patiently, and attentively. I asked for his advice, and surprisingly, I received a letter back. He wrote two pieces of wisdom in his letter that I think about often: "being a pastor is the most context-specific work there is," and "the most dangerous thing is impatience ... keep it slow."

Writing letters to people is deeply contextual. Social media and shared articles go out into the world and can be read across contextual lines, and there is a place for that. But letters bring us back to the local places where God is working among us. They are written to a particular person in a particular place. They are hyper-contextual and that makes them deeply powerful. Personal letters declare that the small, the unseen, the personal, and the kind are values we hold dear. From God's perspective, these activities are never done in vain. In fact, they may be the most life-transforming activities we can engage in. Never underestimate the potency and beauty of deeply context-specific work, like being a pastor with a typewriter.

Going slow is never a waste of time. When we're impatient we can rush past what God may be doing. I've had people come up to me with a hug months after I had written (and forgotten that I had written) them a letter. The slow process of intentional communication doesn't have a built-in immediate response and gratification mechanism. You can't publicly 'like' that I sent you a note. You can only engage in the same intentional way. Slow intentionality builds trust, friendship, and life. It adds the most complex and beautiful flavours.

Letter writers are rediscovering the impact that comes from taking the time to sit down, reflect, write, send off, and wait for a reply. This year for Christmas I gave my seven-year-old niece a package of stamps and a stationary set. Her gift was a year of letter-writing, a kind of pen-pal kit, so she could write back and forth with me. She figured it out in no time, writing me nearly every week with short notes, silly questions, and a few stickers from her sticker collection. We go back and forth and she is such a joy. I find that I'm keeping her tiny artifacts, tender tokens of affection from my little niece. What I thought was a gift for her has become a gift to me.

At its core, letter-writing is the art of giving attention to those people and places that matter to you. It's realizing that your small act of care goes a lot farther that you know. On the day our baby was born, I pulled the anaesthetist aside and thanked him for helping with the labour and delivery. He was amazing and saved the day, in my view. I candidly remarked that he must get hundreds of thank you notes from grateful parents every year! Without missing a beat, he said he had never received a single letter in 20 years. My heart broke. How is it possible that a doctor who had played such a pivotal role in thousands of births, had never received so much as a postcard? I vowed, then and there, to write him a letter, and write more letters to more people, more often. It has been a beautiful journey.

Living relationally in our neighbourhoods requires that we think differently about many of our practices, and try on new practices that could help us engage in the patient way of Jesus within the places where we live. How we speak, write, or care for others reflect what we value and believe to be true about God's work in our midst. What does slow and intentional communication look like between you and your neighbours? In what ways can you reflect the peace of God in the way you speak and encourage others?

Coming Home

The places where we live are more than a collection of houses. Our neighbourhoods are our homes. They are safe havens where kids can run, for families to thrive, and for new relationships to flourish. Each neighbourhood takes on the flavour of the kind of home we hope to create for everyone. Some neighbourhoods are toxic, with social unrest and crime. Yet many more are learning what it means to create a sense of community and togetherness - that feeling of comfort that comes from finding our way home.

On Monday I got a note that there were some swarming bees in another neighbourhood in our city; 20,000 bees were looking for a home. These important, valuable bugs, which are vital to the world we live in, needed to find a resting place. So I tossed my bee veil and sticky leather gloves in the truck and went over to see what was happening. There they were, protecting their queen in a big pile in the mud. With some gentle and careful work we got the bees to safety. By the end of the day, the bees made the move from a pile of weeds in a gravel lot to a beautiful hand-built home that will keep them safe for years. From scattered to gathered. They now live sheltered from storms, safely home.

I'm learning that as a pastor my role is much like this. In a deeply moving way, my work is to help people find their way home. A pastor is someone who sees the small things and reminds the world of their value. We see the crying mother, the newly-in-love teenager, the broken relationship, or the father who is celebrating a new job. We try to spot grace and hope. Pastors point out the beauty in a world where everything is either viewed as functional or worthless. We teach in stories and poetry, bringing God's story to life in our own. A pastor is someone who deeply believes that all creatures, all people and places, need to find a resting place. We believe that God is always at work, gently and carefully leading us to safety, because we are all looking for a home.

At the end of the day a pastor will not be known for what he made, or fixed, or solved, or programatized. Rather pastors are most satisfied in how well they were able to tend to the smallest and the weakest, to the hidden and beautiful things sprouting in our midst. My own attention as a pastor is often drawn to things that may seem strange, or useless. Perhaps our work is only seen from the long view, but evidence of new life can be found all around.

So why do I drop what I am doing to gather up some bees? Shouldn't I be doing more important things with my time or with my life? Well, by some measures, I probably should. But each time I do something virtually inconsequential, such as saving some bees, or meeting with a neighbour, or listening to a hurting community member, I am enacting a prayer, and a deep hope that God never views our lives and our city as inconsequential. Nothing is long-lost in God's eyes, and so they should never be lost in our.

When we each begin to see the small and meaningful moments in our own lives, we, too, become people whose imaginations are being shaped for something more. We become those who point the way 'home.' We become people who comfort those in fear, and remind each other that there is a way through. We all deeply long to be welcomed home with open arms. Who are you welcoming home today?

God works here

There are over 1,100 places named in the Bible. Cities, regions, towns, landmarks, and topographical formations. These locations make up the backdrop, and often become key characters, in the unfolding story of God found in the Bible. Places like Bethlehem may spark our imagination for a baby born in a barn at Christmas time. Jericho might bring back some vague memory of a Sunday school teacher and flannel-graph lesson. Something about falling walls? But in my own experience, many people gloss over the names of places in the Bible stories. Who knows anything about Beth-Shemesh, the Azekah Valley, or the land of Goshen, anyway? Who cares?

One course that I teach often at theological schools is a course in Biblical geography. As a neighbourhood enthusiast and pastor, I am deeply interested in the geography, topography, and localized details of the land where the Biblical stories took place. I have learned that the story of God's people is not set in a vacuum, removed from the dust and pain of real places at a specific time. God's people interacted with God, fought with God, and were loved by God in deserts, caves, lush meadows, busy cities, under oppressive governments, or while trying to grow food in barren land. The Land of the Bible is roughly the size of Vancouver Island or New Jersey and yet it is the place where the story of God unfolded over thousands of years. In this context, place names were more than passing details, they were vital indicators and key markers in a dynamic narrative.

On the first day of any course I teach on Biblical geography, I love watching the students file in. Tired and bored, dreading a class in, what? Geography? Groan. You can see the eyes roll.

For many students, their imaginations are not shaped by place. They live in a digital world, a directionless reality. They can let *Google Maps* find the way, and a street name is non-essential information. Just turn left and right, your phone will get you to where you need to go. So when they're confronted with the book of Samuel in the Bible, rich with geographic details and place names, their eyes glaze over and they pass out. It is expected. Yet, for educators like me, this is a moment I long for: teasing at the edge of an epiphany.

In my Biblical geography class, I often take my students for a stroll through their own neighbourhood. A walk from the grocery story to the McDonalds is the same distance Jesus walked from his trial to his crucifixion. A drive from this neighbourhood to another suburb is roughly how far the Israelites routed out the Philistines after David killed Goliath. With crayons in hand we begin to identify cities, connect towns, highlight roads, and place key characters. In the midst of it all my students are learning something they had never considered: places matter. By the third day, students are shouting out answers and flipping through pages. The story of God, in their imaginations, moves from obscure words in the text to living locations. When these students get a taste of place, they discover that the Bible is not a set of stale precepts; it is an unfolding, dynamic, and engaging account of God, alive and at work in a very real world.

The very same is true for our own neighbourhoods. I am surprised by how few places we visit, on foot, in our own communities. Chestermere is a city built by a lake, yet so few people visit the lake. They drive by but do not stop.

How about the bridge at the south end?
The dog park on the west side?
The beach at the north end?
Surely you know about the new sushi place?

Our neighbourhoods are a collection of place names and streets that people call home. The unique contours and quirky features of our cities are found nowhere else in the world. When we stop to consider how amazing our slice of paradise is, we begin to open the door to see and understand how God feels about the places where we live.

If the story of God, as it unfolds in the Bible, is one marked by place (city, valley, lake, stream, and grove of trees), then how are we to consider the very places that we call home? Could we see God at work shaping the culture and life of our neighbourhoods?

I named this book after my own neighbourhood, Rainbow Falls. My neighbourhood was named this after the manmade waterfalls in the middle of my community. The waterfalls look like real rock, but they're actually spray-painted concrete.The water pump is turned on and off depending on the time of year. The falls are beautiful and it is likely that some consultancy group or advertising firm built their promotional material around this feature - developers want to sell houses and promote their product as best as they can. But the name of my neighbourhood will exist long after the last condo is built and the developer moves on to plough over some other farmland for the very last time.

It is humbling to consider that Rainbow Falls has the potential to become a place name that inspires hope and life, or it may become a sketchy neighbourhood that is the brunt of jokes. To say that you're from Rainbow Falls today means very little. It is a neutral new community, an address on a street sign. It is a suburban development without much backstory and very little culture or history. I mused recently that our neighbourhood should come with little historical plaques mounted on homes and green spaces, celebrating the two-year-old 'history' of our neighbourhood. In reality, its history has not yet been written.

Like a new beehive that has not yet produced honey or a vineyard that was only recently planted, Rainbow Falls does not yet have 'terroir.' It does not have a taste of place.

But it might, one day.

Every small act of place-making we engage in, every time we host a block party, or a barbeque or a kids' soapbox car derby, we are creating culture. We are giving the names of our streets and parks meaning and history. Moment by moment we are saying that our places matter, and the people who live here are creating a true sense of home. Our concrete waterfalls become a gathering place for kids on training wheels, and our cookie-cutter suburban streets and cul-de-sacs become home to annual festivals that are unique in all the world.

God loves Rainbow Falls and the people who live here. God is delighted to add the names of our streets and the names of our families to the list of places where God's story is unfolding. My prayer is that this community will not only have a unique flavour, but also a floral aroma of life and the bright sounds of peace and hope. Rainbow Falls is becoming known as a place where redemption happens, and it's delicious.

Making the Invisible Visible: Taste of Place

Everything we do adds flavour to the places where we live. Our presence is the 'terroir' that people experience. In the same way that high-altitude South American coffee, or French wine, or Scottish whiskey are beloved for their 'terroir,' you have the power to influence the taste of the place where you are living right now. Here are several postures and practices that will help make visible the invisible in your neighbourhood. They will help tease out and add flavour, to the taste of your place.

1. Write letters: During the month of April, letter-writers take up the challenge to write 30 letters in 30 days. These may be simple notes of gratitude after meeting with a friend or neighbour, or it might be a silly note or sketch to a kid you know. When is the last time you've sent a letter to your spouse? It may be a great way to show them how much you love them. Is there someone you know who is driving you crazy? Send them a note and find a way of honestly appreciating their better qualities. Encourage the recipient of your letter to get in on the fun by sending them a self-addressed, stamped envelope along with your letter. There's nothing quite like going to the mailbox and finding a personal letter among the bills and flyers. Whether it's April or not, start writing letters and challenge yourself to engage in slow and intentional ways with the people around you.

2. Celebrate the unique identity of your neighbourhood: Experiment by creating new signage for your neighbourhood, street, or local park. Build a website or start a newsletter that gives the place where you live a particular identity. It has been said that if you want to make something stand out, make a logo for it. As we find ways to make our neighbourhoods unique, we instill a love for the place we live. Soon others will find ways of celebrating the unique flavour of the place you call home.

3. Be hospitable: Nothing changes a story or creates community culture like sharing a meal together. Almost every friendship that has sprouted up in our city can be traced back to a barbeque, block party, or dinner gathering. When we eat, we share in life together. What if you set out to host one monthly meal at your home this year and invited all kinds of unlikely and familiar guests? Imagine what could happen in our home or family if you made this one of your annual goals?

Curates

Husbandry

You'll be known as those who can fix anything,
restore old ruins, rebuild and renovate,
make the community livable again.
-Isaiah 58:12 *(The Message)*

There is a new kind of beehive that has been making waves in the beekeeping community. Current beehives, with their stackable boxes and removable frames, have remained unchanged for 150 years or more. Rev. Lorenzo Langstroth refined and popularized the present-day 'Langstroth Hive' used by beekeepers today around the world. Like the search for the better mousetrap, innovators have sought to try and create a better beehive without much success. Until now, perhaps. The 'Flow-Hive' is a new innovation that allows for beekeepers to gather honey without having to open up the beehive. Promotional videos show a beehive with a faucet and a slow, yellow glistening stream of honey pouring straight into a jar. Never has beekeeping been so easy! Just put bees in, and turn the faucet as needed.

When the 'Flow-Hive' was first revealed, I got calls from would-be beekeepers thrilled by the ease of this invention. "Preston, now I can become a beekeeper! Look how easy this is! You barely have to do anything to get the honey. What do you think?" Beekeepers all over responded alike: we cringed.

The problem is not the technology. The 'Flow-Hive' could very well be the next generation of beehives. Most beekeepers I know are not Luddites. We'll happily embrace a new innovation if it means helping the bees. However this was different. Well-intentioned honey bee enthusiasts, in their excitement for a quick jar of honey, were forgetting a key reality: beekeeping is husbandry.

Animal husbandry is the art and science of caring for creatures who give back to us. As human civilization grew and flourished, we figured out how to give better care to more animals. Cows, chickens, horses, guinea pigs, and honey bees became sources of food for growing villages and cities. Husbandry, however, is quite the opposite of the fast-food grocery store culture most of us experience today. It takes years of forethought, planning, patience, and care to raise the animals that supply our food, and not many people have had this experience. Farmers, for millennia, have innately known the postures necessary for life. Husbandry is about carefulness, tending to the needs of the animals we hope will thrive. It requires concern for the animal's wellbeing. One day the cow or chicken may become a steak or stew, but that does not come from using or abusing the animal. My own grandfather could talk for hours about his herd of cows, and I remember staying up all night with my aunt as her sheep gave birth - experiencing the marvels of this life firsthand. It did not matter the time of day, farmers made their livestock a priority.

But husbandry is about more than maintaining animals in good health for our own benefit. Husbandry also carries a deeper purpose that involves protecting the land and resources for future generations, for the benefit of all. Farming families often have a deep sense of generational resources, passing along the land and animals rather than using them all up.

When we fail to see honey bees though the lens of husbandry, we may also fail to see the ways in which they need care and protection. We cannot forget that they are in our care, worthy of our concern and attention, of our study and focus. They should be the source of our personal interest, not merely for our use - to tap into as we like. I was deeply struck by the importance of this when I visited a large-scale commercial honey operator recently. He surprised me when he said he didn't frankly know that much about bees. He said, "I don't care about bees as much as people might think. I do this for the money. You, on the other hand, love bees, you spend time with them, read about them, and watch them come and go. There's a big difference." When the honey and the money become the focus, animals take a back seat.

As I learned to care for the bees in my own apiary, I also came to reflect on the care I give to my own neighbours. Did I use them for my own benefit, or was I approaching them with a sense of care and concern? It seems odd, perhaps, to think of husbandry in reference to our neighbours. 'Neighbour Husbandry' is not an idea that is likely to take off, but a similar concept may help us reflect on what it means to live with a caring posture towards those in our neighbourhood. Perhaps we are called to become 'Neighbourhood Curates.'

I recently watched "Night at the Museum" with my daughter. In this movie a quiet history museum is magically brought to life, and the night security guard tries his best to bring the chaos under control. With a Tyrannosaurus skeleton running through the galleries and various historical wax figures jumping into the action, the movie becomes a fun and exciting adventure. In the end, the security guard saves the day and finds ways of caring for all of the "come to life" exhibits.

Most museum curators will not have these kinds of exciting, edge-of-your-seat experiences. Yet curators interpret history in creative ways. These are the story-retainers and story-tellers who attend to beautiful artifacts and relay their meaning. They care about gathering and celebrating history, art, culture, and the natural world. Curators create an environment where visitors can learn and engage.

'Curator' comes from the Latin word, *curare* which means, to 'take care.' It's a fitting word for museum curators. They 'take care' of their museum and the stories the museum is telling. This word, *curare* is found in other professions, too. In law, curators are the legal guardians intended to care for minors or ill persons. Church pastors were once called curates because of their role to care for the spiritual wellbeing of people in their church and community.

Today it seems old-fashioned to talk about curates and curators. Yet there is something compelling about those who make it their purpose to care for others and the world around them. Being 'care-full' is a particular quality that is often left to the professionals - the nurses, the doctors, and the social services workers. Yet professionals alone cannot bring about the kind of caring culture we need. John McKnight, author of *Careless Society*, wrote that "it is only in community that we can find care."[65] He's right. When we become the kind of people who care for others in our neighbourhoods, our neighbourhoods become the kinds of places that provide care back to us.

We may be able to care for our neighbours in obvious ways, such as fixing a flat tire or giving a cup of sugar. Yet becoming the curates of our neighbourhoods takes caring to a whole new level. We become people who are alert to what is happening in the neighbourhood, attentive to the environment that we are fostering, the words we use, and the places we share. We care about local school teachers, or whether the barbershop is doing well. We care about the mom walking her kids to the park, and the city staff fixing the sewer system. Curates see the stories that are often missed in passing and find ways to celebrate the good things they see. Pastors are curates because they care for the spiritual wellbeing of people. Museum workers are curates because they care about preserving history. Lawyers are curates because they care about those who are defenceless. Here is something profoundly meaningful as we journey into the places where we live: you can be a neighbourhood curate. You are being invited to care, in small and large ways, for those around you.

Becoming the curator of your neighbourhood may not be like a "Night at the Museum," but I could bet that there is more than a little excitement and adventure around the corner if you begin to look for, and look after, it.

Keeper

God is like a honey bee
Penetrates the soul of me
Dearly draws the sweetness in
Nectar of the meek, love is
He in me and I in him...
-Steve Bell[66]

Keeping bees is an unusual practice. Honey bees are stinging creatures that are not contained or tamed. No amount of discipline, shackles, or training will make them any more or less than what they are. They live according to a pattern, but not according to my will. We are only the keepers of the bees. We set up a home and an environment for them to thrive in, and pour affection and care on them. If we keep them well, they return. If we fail to keep them well, they swarm - they pack up their bags and go. I may be the owner of my bees, yet they are among the freest of any livestock.

Learning the art of *keeping* bees, as opposed to *controlling* bees, was an important early lesson for me. Honey bee colonies may collapse or thrive based on the intervention of the beekeeper, but in a parallel sense, honey bees do all the work in this relationship. They raise their young, forage for food, and build their comb. The beekeeper who holds their apiary with open hands, attentive yet mindful of the freedom that the bees need, will soon enter into the rhythm of this relationship. It is beautiful.

'Cultivate' and 'keep,' are two words and practices that we do not tend to use today. We consume, we use, we expend, and we tweak. We may problem-solve and collaborate, but few of us see the world through this agrarian language. Cultivation takes time, and keeping requires a special kind of attention. They are words that can shape the way we see the places where we live, and shape a faith that is open to care for our neighbours.

The language of cultivating and keeping is found right at the beginning of the Bible. These two words in Hebrew, cultivate ['abad] and keep [shamar] are found in Genesis 2:15. Here we read about Adam, this first man and the world's first gardener. God asked him to relate to this special paradise garden of Eden with a particular posture. In the ESV we read, "The Lord God took the man and put him in the garden of Eden to till it and keep it." Adam was invited to be a keeper of the garden. It was a core posture that God shaped in Adam, and it sets the tone for how we ought to view the world we inhabit.

However it did not take long for the full-on abandonment of this invitation to be a 'keeper' to take place. In Genesis 4, Adam's sons, Cain and Abel, face off and Cain kills Abel. God confronted Cain, asking him, "Where is Abel?" Cain simply shrugged and replied, "I do not know; am I my brother's keeper?" (Genesis 4:9, ESV). Cain's flippant comment shows the extent of his fractured heart. From one called to tend and keep to passing off this responsibility as though it was nothing. However, Cain's words echo the sentiments of our own hearts. When we hear of sorrow or suffering around the world, let alone in our own cities and neighbourhoods, we turn around almost as if to say, "I don't know. Am I my neighbourhood's keeper?" We may not be complicit in the ills affecting our city, but God takes them seriously. From Jesus we learn that God is deeply interested in the wellbeing of people, so much so that God came to this broken, unkept world, embracing fractured hearts that we might see what love looks like and respond. It is because of Jesus that we are able to say, "I am my brother's keeper." We have the resources we need to be that person. Jesus is tending to the sorrow and gathering 'keepers' like you and me to be what Adam was called to be.

This Old Testament word for 'keeper' is used elsewhere in the Bible. It is used to describe the work of the priests as they served and guarded the temple.[67] The Temple was the place where God's people met with God in a particular way. The Temple and the priests serving there were to be a reminder that God was redeeming the world and bringing life to all things. Priests were called to play a role in telling that story in the way they served and guarded, or *kept*, the temple. They were Temple-keepers, as well as keepers of this amazing, cosmic, redemptive story. Yet even here something changes. The New Testament unfolds a new narrative exploring how we the people are the temple of God (1 Corinthians 3:16). God's Spirit is living in us and we become those who participate with God in this redemptive story. Instead of going to the Temple to become right with God, God's people, through Jesus, are going into the world to bring hope and life wherever they go. The Bible even says that we are priests, those who take this 'keeping' role seriously by living out the grand story of God's redemptive work in the very places we live, work, and play.

Jesus, interestingly, is called the New Adam. He is taking all that is broken and making it beautiful and whole again; he is restoring the work of the 'keeper' and calling us to do the same. Somewhere along the way, in a backyard apiary in Rainbow Falls, Jesus invited me to join him too. Moment by moment, I am simply learning to say 'yes' to God's invitation to keep, guard, restore, care for, and serve those who live near me.

It seems to me we're 'keeping' a lot more than bees.

Becoming a Pastor-Gardener

I heard about a church that had put out a call for a new pastor. When a church is looking for a new pastor they will, among other things, ask for references. Typically these references are other pastors, other churches, and other respected and notable figures. The church in this story, however, was not looking for a typical pastor. This church was looking for something more (and less).

The church, in their search process, asked pastoral candidates to submit the names and phone numbers of all of the pastor's immediate neighbours. The references were the people who had lived next door to the pastor - the people they might run into each day. The church felt that these references, the neighbours, would give them the best possible picture of their future pastor. They wanted the kind of pastor that they'd love to have as a next-door neighbour, and the rest would be built upon that. It was a bold and unusual way of deciding who their pastor would be.

Often when I share this story with groups of pastors, foul flags are tossed from corners of the room. "Whoa there!" Some pastors have built their career on leading a church, running programs, and delivering pitch-perfect sermons. Now they have to be good neighbours, too? Many simply don't have time for that. For other pastors, there is a sense of relief. The ill-fitting clothes of performance reviews and the fatigue of keeping the programs going was never what some pastors imagined. For those who stepped into a life of ministry, called by Jesus to love God with their whole being, and to love their neighbours as themselves, this new metric is like a breath of fresh air.

At Lake Ridge Community Church, where I am one of the pastors, we will often have people approach us, interested in leading a small group, or starting a new ministry, or heading up some project. Typically I'd be excited to take up offers like these, and I would jump at the chance to 'plug in' new volunteers in this way. But I'm learning that people are not plugs, and churches are not receptacles. Mechanical metaphors simply don't reflect the life and rhythms of church and discipleship. I am learning that those who step up to lead may not be those who we need to lead at this time. So I have come to set a different standard for those who ask to lead a group or ministry project. I thank them for offering to serve, and ask them if they would first be willing to host five dinner parties at their home, spend time around their neighbours' tables, and make half-a-dozen coffee dates with people in the community. Some take me up on the offer, and go on to foster rich and authentic work in our midst. Some scoff quietly; their journey takes much longer.

When I was first called to Lake Ridge Community Church, the church was still very much in its infancy. It was a new church plant with a handful of committed leaders who loved the town of Chestermere, and were shaping some beautiful conversations. In the call process, I was asked if my wife and I would have lunch with three people who were very new to the church and were newer followers of Jesus who had no experience in "formal" pastoral interviews. We didn't have an interview, we ate together, laughed, told stories, and talked long about Jesus. The rest is history. Not only did they play a big role in deciding whether I would be their pastor, but they recount that in that moment something also changed in them: they too felt a new level of connection. It was one of the most memorable and beautiful experiences for me, and it set the tone for how I would be a pastor in their midst.

The pastors and leaders we want and need are those who have learned to be loving neighbours, who sit for hours around each other's tables, and who create space for making their neighbourhood beautiful. Every year, when my honey bees emerge from a long, cold Alberta winter, and the garden is springing back to life, I take my cue and dial back my office work on behalf of the church. I get out. I reconnect with neighbours, host barbecues, dig in the garden, spend afternoons walking through my neighbourhood, and find every excuse to be with the people around me. We throw block parties with the new and old friends on our street, and with the kids we create lively old-fashioned soapbox car races down the only hill in our neighbourhood. It is in these warm summer days that I feel like a pastor. It is in being on the porch with neighbours, bees swooping past, dirt under the nails, in ripped jeans, that I see again the pace and posture of the pastoral calling.

This "Pastor Next Door" metric resets the current paradigm and rethinks how we measure pastoral success. In my context, my work is measured not by how many programs I can keep running or how big our next event could be. Our leadership team genuinely celebrates when we're in the neighbourhood, being present and attentive. My preaching is shaped by experiences in my neighbourhood, my pastoral care is informed by the issues facing our small city, and my own family life is shaped by how we engage with other busy families in our community.

As we place value on how engaged our pastors are in their neighbourhoods, we don't lose 'productivity' or 'efficiency,' as some might contend. Something better is happening. Just the other day, in the ice cream shop, a mother recognized me and wanted to chat. In the tattoo shop I discovered I knew almost everyone. The barbers are friends, and the people who run a local store wanted some help with an idea they had. My next door neighbour offers business services to a church member who built my deck, and the friend who built my deck plays in a band along with my other neighbour on Thursday nights. The intricate mix of friendships and neighbourhood connections starts to look less like a program and a calendar of events, and more like a network, a community, and a church.

It is in these places of interpersonal relationships, in the shared joys and sorrows, anger and rest, where we as pastors are being called to reside. It's here that we notice, almost as a surprise, that our church is growing, that people are coming to live like Jesus, and (who would have guessed?) they're also finding that they, too, want to love their neighbours. What is modelled in the life of the pastor, and in church leaders often informs the shapes and contours of the community we serve.

Life sprouts with pastor-gardeners, less with pastor-programmers. Years ago a large church asked me to come and join their staff as a director. I sat in a big office and listened. They talked about how I was going to be a gear in the mechanism of their church, a cog in this well-oiled machine. They were building an edifice fit for God, and I was invited to pull on the levers with them. Yet as I sat there listening to this impressive speech, I remembered something. I was taught years ago to listen for metaphors. Metaphors reveal the true heart, and the heart of this organization was deeply mechanical. I heard nothing about the kind of pastoral work I longed to embrace, to cultivate relationships, water new sprouts, plant hope, and weed out distractions. How could I see and hear the people I was to care for from the cockpit of a bulldozer. This world needs people who are at home out in the garden. As the conversation ended, and the paperwork pushed across the desk with a pen and a smile, I politely declined and walked away.

Programs can never replace the kind of care that the world needs. Our neighbourhoods require people who are willing and able to step into the complex and messy cycles of growth and loss happening all around them.

Neighbourhood Manifesto

Creating an amazing city or neighbourhood is less about a silver bullet solution and more about rediscovering a lost art. A neighbourhood manifesto helps us see with new focus the ways in which we are all invited to bring life to the places where we live. New language can inspire us to nurture community and aspire to create a dynamic, thriving city of abiding hope and grace. As you seek to care for others, may you find inspiration in my neighbourhood manifesto:

We're for Facebook mentions that lead to face-to-face connections.
We're for listening to stories and creating memories.
We're not afraid of crisis or pain, it will come; we're in this together.
We're expecting mistakes. Grace is the cornerstone of our city.
We're for hand-delivered cards, not trading barbs.
We're for sharing our barbeque steak and our Kraft Dinner. There's always room at the table.
We're for loving enemies and making allies.
We're for surprising our neighbours with fresh hot biscuits, not bylaw tickets.
We're for kids; we slow down and we get to know them.
We're for joining in whatever is already happening, cheering good things along.
We're more than residents or citizens, we're neighbours.
We're sure that making our neighbourhoods welcoming places will always be the better way.
We're for generosity experiments and sneaky acts of kindness.
We're for throwing snowballs and block parties, not tantrums or tirades.

We're for bringing the best out in others and for being in our neighbour's corner.

We're for forgiveness.

We're for waiting when patience is needed.

We're discovering that the best security system is a well-connected neighbourhood.

We're setting the DNA of our city – even now.

We're here for a purpose. Our neighbourhood is better because we're in it.

We're for celebrating what we have, not angry about what we don't.

We're sure that the small things are important. In fact they may be the most important.

We're for our teachers, our firefighters, our politicians, our barbers, and our tattoo artists.

We're neighbourhood environmentalists who create space for growth.

We're for creating cultures of trust.

We're discovering that a neighbourhood is more like a garden and less like a veneer.

We're convinced the people around us are amazing, unique, rare, and eternally valuable.

We're for solving problems over coffee, not over a pitchfork.

We're fluent in the language of potlucks, garden parties, and impromptu marshmallow roasts.

We're for good ideas and the courage to see them happen.

We're sure we can do this together.

This is my Neighbourhood Manifesto

Making the Invisible Visible: Curates

Curates are those who care for the big picture. They hear the stories, preserve a memory, they embrace the lonely, and celebrate when something good happens. All of this cannot be done in a vacuum. Caring neighbours are those who step into the mess and see life in a garden where others may only see weeds. How might you become a neighbourhood curate?

1. Words: The things we say have power to build up or destroy. Becoming a caregiver in the neighbourhood is shaped largely by the words we say, and those words come from a heart shaped to be attentive. This week, listen to the words you use to describe your neighbours. Are they disparaging or sarcastic, or are they creating a new culture of life in the place where you live?

2. Neighbourhood walk: Take time to walk through your neighbourhood. Find the back alleys and pathways, linger in a parking lot and find new places to explore. Look around. Is your neighbourhood being cared for? Are there signs of life or loss? Take time to write down what you see, and if you are able, revisit your notes in a year. Has the small and consistent work of care you have provided changed anything in your neighbourhood?

3. Guerrilla gardening: We've often dreamt of planting flowers or shrubs in neglected places in our city. The idea of secretly creating a garden in the middle of the night for people to enjoy the next day has always appealed to us. How could you do a secret act of caring in a way that surprises and brings hope to your neighbourhood?

4. Transactional neighbours: Create a list of your neighbours, and consider the kind of connections you have with them. How many of them are transactional and how many are relational? This may take some deeper reflection. Transactional neighbours are those who provide us with some benefit. It is a consumer connection. While relational neighbours are those whom we value just as they are and often at a cost to us. Are there neighbours you avoid because they do not benefit you at all? How could you create more meaningful (and caring) relationships in your neighbourhood?

5. Read 1 Peter 2:5 and reflect on how we are called to be "living stones" and "holy priests." What does it mean to be those who reflect the presence of God in the places where we live, and serve as 'keepers,' attentive to the wellbeing of those around us?

Conclusion

A few weeks ago I wrapped up my beehives with insulation and black thick plastic. Honey bees do not hibernate, they huddle together, buzz softly, and wait out the long, cold, and dark Canadian winter. There is a rhythm to beekeeping and my part in this dance is to help them prepare for this new season. Even now I sit and look out over these frost-covered hives. I feel for them and the long wait ahead.

Honey bees do not live very long, perhaps a couple months during the summer. Honey bees that are born in the late autumn live a little longer. Their job is to keep the hive warm all winter and then nurture the first spring bees as they emerge. Bees born in the fall die off before the first flowers bloom in the spring. They will never see or taste a blossom. They call these the winter bees.

Imagine what it must be like to be a winter bee. To feel this desire to fly, but never go beyond the front door. To know the urge to hop from flower to flower, but never taste warm summer nectar for yourself. To have eyes that see in vibrant floral shades of ultraviolets, blues, and yellows, but only experience darkness. We know that without the winter bees, the hive would not survive. Without the winter bees, the world would not survive. Even in the dead of winter the honey bees whose job it is to keep the hive warm remain a vital keystone species. We know that the honey bee who never experiences the blazing summer sun is as beautiful and awe-inspiring as the one zipping through our gardens in July. We know that a honey bee is a honey bee is a honey bee.

We feel for them - the winter bees who wait.

In my own neighbourhood we settle in to our long winters and sometimes we carry our own darkness. We may experience challenges and difficulties at work or at home. We may labour under stresses and carry sorrows that others might never see. Deep down we might wonder if we were made for something more, if perhaps under different circumstances we could do more - be something more. We doubt. We crave flavours of life and love that we know must exist, but have yet to taste for ourselves. And then, when it's still and calm, we wonder if there is a world beyond what we know.

Paul, in the Bible, wrote that the whole world is like a woman groaning in birth pangs. "All around us we observe a pregnant creation. The difficult times of pain throughout the world are simply birth pangs. But it's not only around us; it's within us. The Spirit of God is arousing us within. We're also feeling the birth pangs" (Romans 8:22, *The Message*). This groaning, this yearning, this deep sense that there has got to be something more, is God's Spirit reminding us: we are who God says we are. We are beloved. We are mind-bogglingly unique. We are gifted. We are called and invited. We are partners with God. We are able to make this world anew. We are keystone people who are vital to the wellbeing of our neighbourhoods and cities. We are being prepared to move, to step out, and to come alive.

God knows this is true of us. God started this story and foreknew our part in it. We were made for this. It's in our bones. In our darkness we may not see this, but we feel the urge, the instinct, the taste of a sun-bright-flower-burst-garden-life just beyond our imaginations. There is something happening here. People, families, communities, and neighbourhoods (including people like me and you) are learning to live into God's vision of paradise. God is revealing that the aroma of heaven, this 'land of milk and honey,' is found in the very places we live - where *you* live.

Winter is over.

The first blooms are ready.
And it's very possible that you are, too.

Appendix

and Resources

Keystone People Worksheet

Keystone people are those who see themselves as participants in God's big story for the places where they live. They play a pivotal role. It is a useful metaphor for thinking about the role we play in our neighbourhoods. Think of this resource as a tool to help you reflect on the ways you may be bringing life to your community, or reflect on how you may just be passing through.

Keystone People	Passing Through People
I am living in a public sphere. It's for me and those around me.	My living space is enclosed. It's for me and my close friends.
My resources build a longer table to welcome others.	My resources build a higher fence to keep me safe.
I am steeped in who God says I am.	I am steeped in who I think I am.
I seek to find out where God is at work here and now.	I believe God is mostly at work somewhere else.
I find small things important.	I dismiss the small as unimportant.
I know how to slow down to discover	I believe moving slow is lazy and

what God is doing.	useless.
I know God is leading. I trust the Spirit.	I have a personal master-plan.
I see the whole neighbourhood as God's arena of hope and redemption.	I see the Church alone as the place where God is at work.
I am focused on my neighbours, whoever they may be.	I am focused on my affinity group and ethnicity.
I value the Kingdom and see my neighbourhood through Jesus's parables.	I value my own kingdom and see the world through my own lens.
I believe my neighbourhood can change and so I step in bravely with Jesus.	I believe little can change, and so I retreat.
I believe God is already here.	I invite God, but God may or may not show up.
I know God's people, and People of Peace can be found all around me.	I am alone in this.
My neighbourhood is a place that is teaching me how to follow Jesus.	My neighbourhood is incidental to my journey of faith in Jesus.
I want to hear God say, "Well done, you trusted in me."	I want to hear God say, "Well done, you overachiever!"
The joy I am looking for is found with Jesus right where I am.	The joy I am looking for isn't found on this earth.
I'll only be satisfied when I am trusting in Jesus wherever I am.	I'll only be satisfied when I'm doing what I want to do.

I am a gardener. I create an environment for growth all around me. I am a creator.	I use what I see around me for my own purposes. I am a consumer.
I relate to those around me, enjoying the transformations I see.	I transact with those around me, wondering how I can benefit.
I leave space in my life for spontaneity and availability.	I am so busy, I have no time for others.
I crave life, so I look for beauty all around me and find that I am awoken by God's goodness.	I find life hard, so I retreat to my own diversion to numb the pain.
I foster a culture of trust and find my neighbours are allies - so I open my life to them.	I am afraid and think my neighbours are a risk to me - so I close my life to them.
I think my neighbourhood and the people around me are amazing - created by God, wow!	I think my neighbourhood is a collection of buildings and the people are in the way, whatever.

Endnotes

[1] Thérèse, *The Autobiography of Saint Thérèse of Lisieux: The Story of a Soul* (New York, NY: Image Books/Doubleday, 2001), 163.

[2] Alasdair MacIntyre, *Dependent Rational Animals* (London: Duckworth, 1999), 1.

[3] Thérèse, *The Autobiography of Saint Thérèse of Lisieux: The Story of a Soul* (New York, NY: Image Books/Doubleday, 2001), 163.

[4] Corey Kilgannon, "The Queen of Green," The New York Times, December 6, 2015, MB4.

[5] Margot Harris, "Meet The Green Lady Who's Always Dressed For St. Paddy's Day," Distractify, March 17, 2016, accessed July 15, 2016, http://distractify.com/trending/2016/03/17/the-green-woman.

[6] John Lynch, Bill Thrall, and Bruce McNicol, *On My Worst Day* (San Clemente, CA: CrossSection, 2013), 106.

[7] John Lynch, Bill Thrall, and Bruce McNicol, *On My Worst Day* (San Clemente, CA: CrossSection, 2013), 51.

[8] Bockmuehl, Markus. "Strawberries, the Food of Paradise." Crux 27, no. 3 (September 1991): 16.

[9] David Badke, "Fox," The Medieval Bestiary January 15, 2011, accessed August 16, 2015, http://bestiary.ca/beasts/beast179.htm.

[10] Bockmuehl, Markus. "Strawberries, the Food of Paradise." Crux 27, no. 3 (September 1991): 16.

[11] David Badke, "Bestiary of Anne Walshe," The Medieval Bestiary (blog), April 17, 2001, accessed August 16, 2016, http://bestiary.ca/articles/anne_walshe/index.html.

[12] David Badke, "Bee," The Medieval Bestiary January 15, 2011, accessed August 16, 2016, http://bestiary.ca/beasts/beast260.htm.

[13] C. Marina. Marchese, *Honeybee: Lessons from an Accidental Beekeeper* (New York: Black Dog & Leventhal Publishers, 2011), 100.

[14] G. Bloch et al., "Industrial Apiculture in the Jordan Valley during Biblical times with Anatolian Honeybees," Proceedings of the National Academy of Sciences 107, no. 25 (2010): , doi:10.1073/pnas.1003265107.

[15] "Rosslyn Chapel Was Haven for Bees," BBC News, March 30, 2010, accessed September 14, 2015, http://news.bbc.co.uk/2/hi/uk_news/scotland/8594724.stm.

[16] "Rosslyn Chapel Was Haven for Bees," BBC News, March 30, 2010, accessed September 14, 2015, http://news.bbc.co.uk/2/hi/uk_news/scotland/8594724.stm.

[17] "Bees Cause a Buzz at Chapel | The Official Rosslyn Chapel Website," The Official Rosslyn Chapel Website, June 15, 2015, accessed August 15, 2016, http://www.rosslynchapel.com/news/bees-cause-a-buzz-at-chapel/.

[18] Thérèse, *The Autobiography of Saint Thérèse of Lisieux: The Story of a Soul* (New York, NY: Image Books/Doubleday, 2001), 3.

[19] Dan White, Jr., "Confessing Church Planters Guilt," July 20, 2015, accessed August 15, 2015, http://danwhitejr.blogspot.ca/2015/07/confessing-church-planters-guilt.html?m=1.

[20] H. Storch, *At the Hive Entrance, European Apiculture Editions*, 1985, 5.

[21] Emily Dickinson and Helen Vendler, Dickinson: *Selected Poems and Commentaries* (Harvard University Press, 2010), 522.

[22] Mandy Smith, *The Vulnerable Pastor: How Human Limitations Empower Our Ministry* (Downers Grove, IL: InterVarsity Press, 2015), 195.

[23] Christopher J. H. Wright, *The Mission of God: Unlocking the Bible's Grand Narrative* (Downers Grove, IL: IVP Academic, 2006), 219.

[24] C. Baxter Kruger, *God is For Us* (Jackson, MS: Perichoresis Press, 2000), 21.

[25] Ibid., 22.

[26] David Morgan, *The Embodied Eye: Religious Visual Culture and the Social Life of Feeling* (Berkeley: University of California Press, 2012), 70.

[27] *C.S. Lewis, Christian* Reflections (Grand Rapids, MI: Wm B. Eerdmans Publishing, 2014), 208.

28 B. W. Urban, "Concepts and Correlations Relevant to General Anaesthesia," British Journal of Anaesthesia 89, no. 1 (2002): 3-16.

29 Eugene H. Peterson et al., *Subversive Spirituality* (Grand Rapids, MI: W.B. Eerdmans, 1997), 13.

30 Barbara Brown. Taylor, *An Altar in the World: A Geography of Faith* (New York: HarperOne, 2009), 172.

31 Hall, Daryl, and John Oates. *Rich Girl.* Hall & Oates. Christopher Bond, 1976. Vinyl recording.

32 Fyodor Dostoevsky, *The Idiot*, trans. Constance Garnett (New York: Bantam, 1981), 370.

33 Hans Urs Von Balthasar, John Kenneth. Riches, and Joseph Fessio, *Seeing the Form: The Glory of the Lord: A Theological Aesthetics* (San Francisco: Ignatius Press, 1982), 33.

34 Malcolm Guite and Fraser N. Watts, *Sounding the Seasons: Seventy Sonnets for the Christian Year* (Norwich: Canterbury Press, 2012), 54.

35 Henri J. M. Nouwen, *Behold the Beauty of the Lord: Praying with Icons* (Notre Dame, IN: Ave Maria Press, 1987), 33.

36 Eugene Peterson. *Practice Resurrection: A Conversation on Growing Up in Christ.* Grand Rapids: Eerdmans, 2010. 139.

37 Maggie Stuckey. *Soup Night.* North Adams, MA: Storey, 2013.

38 Mary Oliver, *Why I Wake Early: New Poems* (Boston: Beacon Press, 2004), 67.

39 Michele Berger, "Penn Psychologists Study Intense Awe Astronauts Feel Viewing Earth From Space," Penn News, April 18, 2016, accessed May 10, 2016, https://news.upenn.edu/news/penn-psychologists-study-intense-awe-astronauts-feel-viewing-earth-space.

40 David B. Yaden et al., "The Overview Effect: Awe and Self-transcendent Experience in Space Flight.," Psychology of Consciousness: Theory, Research, and Practice 3, no. 1 (2016): 3.

41 Frederick Buechner, Beyond Words: Daily Readings in the ABC's of Faith (New York: HarperSanFrancisco, 2004), 291-292.

42 "Bees' Tiny Brains Beat Computers, Study Finds," The Guardian, October 24, 2010, accessed April 09, 2016, https://www.theguardian.com/world/2010/oct/24/bees-route-finding-problems.

[43] Eugene H. Peterson, *Under the Unpredictable Plant* (Grand Rapids, MI: Eerdmans, 1992) 60.

[44] Ali Binazir, "What Are the Chances of Your Coming into Being?," Ali Binazir, 2011, accessed October 20, 2015, http://blogs.harvard.edu/abinazir/2011/06/15/what-are-chances-you-would-be-born/.

[45] Vincent van Gogh. *Letter to Theo van Gogh*. Written c. 17 September 1888 in Arles. Translated by Mrs. Johanna van Gogh-Bonger, edited by Robert Harrison, number 538. URL: http://webexhibits.org/vangogh/letter/18/538.htm.

[46] Lewis B. Smedes, *Mere Morality: What God Expects from Ordinary People* (Grand Rapids, MI: W.B. Eerdmans Pub., 1983), 106.

[47] "Corruption by Country: Indonesia," Transparency International, accessed January 20, 2016, http://www.transparency.org/country#IDN.

[48] "Corruption Continues to Plague Indonesia," Gallup, accessed August 15, 2016, http://www.gallup.com/poll/157073/corruption-continues-plague-indonesia.aspx.

[49] Norimitsu Onishi, "Making Honesty a Policy in Indonesia Cafes," The New York Times, June 15, 2009, accessed November 18, 2015, http://www.nytimes.com/2009/06/16/world/asia/16indo.html?_r=0.

[50] John McKnight and Peter Block, *The Abundant Community: Awakening the Power of Families and Neighborhoods* (Chicago: American Planning Association, 2010), 19.

[51] Kenneth E. Bailey, *Jesus through Middle Eastern Eyes: Cultural Studies in the Gospels* (Downers Grove, IL: IVP Academic, 2008), 293, 295.

[52] Mark Labberton, *The Dangerous Act of Loving Your Neighbor: Seeing Others through the Eyes of Jesus* (Downers Grove, IL: IVP Books, 2010), 44.

[53] Ibid., 47.

[54] Elizabeth W. Dunn and Michael Norton, "Hello, Stranger," The New York Times, April 27, 2014, SR6 sec., April 25, 2014, http://www.nytimes.com/2014/04/26/opinion/sunday/hello-stranger.html?_r=0.

[55] Elizabeth Lawrence and Bill Neal, *Through the Garden Gate* (Chapel Hill: University of North Carolina Press, 2000), 142.

[56] British Psychological Society (BPS). "Being bored at work can make us more creative." ScienceDaily.

www.sciencedaily.com/releases/2013/01/130108201517.htm (accessed August 4, 2016).

[57] Hannah Richardson, "Children Should Be Allowed to Get Bored, Expert Says," BBC News, March 23, 2013, accessed July 20, 2016, http://www.bbc.com/news/education-21895704.

[58] Psalm 40:1, 3, NLT

[59] Galatians 5:22-23, NLT

[60] "The Case for Boredom," WNYC (blog), January 12, 2015, accessed August 29, 2015, http://www.wnyc.org/story/bored-brilliant-project-part-1/.

[61] Kari Leibowitz, "The Norwegian Town Where the Sun Doesn't Rise," The Atlantic, July 1, 2015, accessed January 12, 2016, http://www.theatlantic.com/health/archive/2015/07/the-norwegian-town-where-the-sun-doesnt-rise/396746/#disqus_thread.

[62] Linnet, Jeppe Trolle (2011). "Money can't buy me hygge: Danish middle-class consumption, egalitarianism and the sanctity of inner space". Social Analysis: Journal of Cultural and Social Practice. 55, 2, p. 21-44

[63] Anne Lamott, *Plan B: Further Thoughts on Faith* (New York, NY: Penguin Group, 2005), 46.

[64] Roger Draper, "Will the Pope Change the Vatican or Will the Vatican Change the Pope?," National Geographic, August 2015, 51.

[65] John McKnight, *The Careless Society: Community and Its Counterfeits* (New York: BasicBooks, 1995), 172.

[66] Steve Bell. *Ever Present Need.* Steve Bell, Dave Zeglinski, 2003, CD. Original poem by St. Francis of Assisi.

[67] Oren R. Martin, *Bound for the Promised Land: The Land Promise in God's Redemptive Plan* (Downers Grove, IL: InterVarsity Press, 2015), 37.

Acknowledgements

Thank you to many friends and family who edited and responded to the early drafts of this book: Eleanor Beck, Dixie Vandersluys, Alison Leontaridis, Karen Albertson, Jennifer Peddlesden, Mark Pouteaux, Lee Woolery, and Rohadi Nagassar.

Thank you to Stephen Burris and his team at Urban Loft Publishers for welcoming this project and encouraging its development.

Thanks to Lake Ridge Community Church, the beautiful saints in Chestermere who daily live out their faith in Jesus in remarkable ways. It is a joy and honour to serve with you as your pastor. A very special thank you to Evan Dewald, my co-pastor and partner in joining in whatever God is doing in our city. You are a dear friend and brother.

Thank you to the Forge Canada team, to Cam Roxburgh, Karen Wilk, Anthony Brown, Howard Lawrence, Rainer Kunz, and Merv Budd who encouraged me to write this book, and who open doors for missional communities to connect and flourish across our country.

Thank you to those who, early on, endorsed this book. Thank you to Michael Frost, Alan Hirsch, Lyndon Penner, Michelle Sanchez, Eric Samuel Timm, and

Steve Bell. Thank you for seeing the project as a meaningful contribution to the conversations we all share together.

Thank you to my fellow collaborators in *Rainbow Falls* who make loving our neighbourhood a delight: the Nelsons, the Pollards, the Peases, the Kindrets, the Bauhuises, the Gaddis, the Tarrants, the Bergers, the Eldessoukis, the Hamiltons, and so many others. I love having you as neighbours!

Thanks to my beekeeping community. To Peter Beermann for taking me under his wing and starting the chain of events that led to writing this book. To the Chestermere Honey Bee Society, each of you are crazy wonderful.

I wish to express my deepest gratitude for my family. For my parents, Vic and Brenda Pouteaux, who demonstrated deep hospitality in our home, and to my sister Andrea and brother-in-law Darcy Durksen who live with such tangible love for their neighbours. Also to my mother-in-law, Barb Miller, for filling our home with peace and joy.

Most of all I want to thank my wife, Kelly, whose tender example of love for me and all who cross our path is a reflection of Jesus. You are my ally.

About the Author

Dr. Preston Pouteaux is a beekeeper, neighbourhood enthusiast, and pastor at Lake Ridge Community Church. He is an engaging speaker, writer, and curator of conversations about faith and neighbourhoods. He serves nationally with Forge Canada and teaches at colleges across the country. He studied at Covenant Bible College, Briercrest College, Regent College, Tyndale Seminary, and Jerusalem University College in Israel. He is the author of *Imago Dei to Missio Dei* [VantagePoint3]. Since 2015 his syndicated column, Into the Neighbourhood, has been printed over one million times in weekly newspapers. Preston lives in Chestermere, Alberta, with his wife Kelly, their daughters Scotia and Ivy, and a few thousand honeybees.

Manufactured by Amazon.ca
Bolton, ON